THE SEXUAL EXPLOITATION
OF CHILDREN

THE SEXUAL EXPLOITATION
OF CHILDREN

Judith Ennew

Polity Press

© Judith Ennew, 1986.

First published 1986 by Polity Press, Cambridge, in association with
Basil Blackwell, Oxford.

Editorial Office:
Polity Press, Dales Brewery, Gwydir Street, Cambridge CB1 2LJ, UK.

Basil Blackwell Ltd, 108 Cowley Road, Oxford OX4 1JF, UK.

British Library Cataloguing in Publication Data

Ennew, Judith
   The sexual exploitation of children
   1. Child molesting
   I. Title
   362.7'044   HQ71

ISBN 0-7456-0230-4
ISBN 0-7456-0231-2 Pbk

Typeset by Fotoset (Typesetting Services) Oxon.

Printed and bound in Great Britain
by Billing & Sons Limited, Worcester.

There is an elementary sexuality which is innocent, and there is an elementary sexuality which is morally and aesthetically squalid.
Aldous Huxley, *The Devils of Loudun*

Contents

Acknowledgements

My professional interest in the sexual exploitation of children arose through the studies of working children with which I have been associated since 1979. While researching a report for the United Kingdom Overseas Development Administration in the Peruvian capital city of Lima, I studied child prostitution among other kinds of juvenile street occupations. In 1984, I was commissioned by the Anti-Slavery Society to write a report on child prostitution and pornography for UNICEF. The present book is the outcome of some of this work, using material and arguments which I was unable to incorporate into the UNICEF report. I am indebted to all my former colleagues in the Anti-Slavery Society, to Bo Carlsson of Radda Barnen and Nigel Cantwell of Defence for Children International for their help with earlier work. I am particularly grateful to Sheena Crawford, who was my research assistant on that report, for her interest, insights and friendship while I was writing it. A particularly lively session of the Saturday Seminar Society in Cambridge gave an opportunity to discuss some of the ideas, and the comments of Duffy Breese and Maryon McDonald were especially helpful. Brian Milne and Christine Robinson have provided additional material and John Ash, Jill Korbin and Eileen Vizard read earlier drafts and gave invaluable advice and encouragement. Brian Milne was responsible for all the graphics and I am grateful to Eileen Vizard for permission to use the table in figure 3.

The opinions expressed in this report are my own and the book is intended to be read as a discussion document. I cannot pretend to have all, or even any, of the answers. What I have tried to do is present the material in ways which avoid both sensationalism and prior judgements. Of course I have my prejudices and where possible I have tried to make these explicit. I have deliberately suppressed the names of publi-

cations and agencies which produce or distribute pornographic material apart from that easily available in high street
outlets. This is in order to discourage any chance prurient
readership.

Cambridge, August 1985

Introduction

This book has more to say about power than about sex. It is therefore also about the abuse of power and the powerlessness of particular categories of person. In general, the powerless group I examine consists of children. But it is clear that other categorizations like class, race and gender also play their part in exploitative relations between adults and children. Sexual exploitation is one form of exploitation among others, taking its place in the schemata of power relationships along with those in the labour market, in the family, in education and politics as well as many others. In the following pages readers will find very little to feed their imaginings about sexual practices between adults and children. There will be no suitably disguised examples of child pornography. My main concern is to analyse the sets of ideas and social structures within which child sexual exploitation exists, both as a practice and as a problem.

Practice and problem are treated separately here because, to a certain extent, they are independent of each other. The range of possible adult–child sexual activities differs little between different places and times, even though the incidence may vary. But attitudes vary a great deal. There have been, and still are, subgroups in many societies which view sexual relationships between adult males and young boys not only as permissible but also as desirable, because they represent the highest form of romantic love. It is clear that both Plato and Plutarch, to name two well-known examples, were of this opinion. There are other examples of cultures which suppress any knowledge or discussion of child sexuality and may combine this with rigid ideologies of adult sexual morality. Some groups wish to liberate children from what they see as repressive moral systems. Others wish to protect children from sexual experiences and from bearing any other kind of adult responsibility. These groups may also initiate moral campaigns which publicize child sexual exploitation, claiming that it is the outcome of a general moral and social malaise.

This type of moral crusade has been evident in the United Kingdom and the United States of America in varying strengths over at least the past two decades. Changes in sexual mores during the past four decades have aroused fear as well as relief at the breakdown of former rigid values. Some social groups have reacted by challenging new individual freedoms in the field of sexuality in the name of a set of reborn or rehabitated absolute moral values. According to socialist historian Jeffrey Weeks

> The new absolutism has many affinities with the old – it is often rooted in the same fundamentalist religious values – but its new gloss stems from a fashionable flirtation with sociobiological speculations about our 'true' human nature, and from a contingent affinity with certain trends within radical feminism (particularly its hostility to pornography and violence). (Weeks 1985, p. 28)

In an interview in 1980, Judith Bat-Ada blamed 'saturation with straightforward sexual stimulus' for an increased social interest in other forms of stimulus, such as sex with children or with animals and sexual violence (Lederer 1980). Saturation appears to be related to an increased interest in sex for recreational purpose – 'purely for fun in any form which is found pleasurable and exciting, as sex is more and more dissociated from procreation' (Rossman 1979). Why the practice of 'sex for fun' should lead first to saturation and then to dissatisfaction with 'normal' forms of heterosexual activity is not clear. It might be just as logical to assume that the satiated individual would become bored with any kind of sexual activity and try alternative non-sexual forms of recreation. After all this is what happens in many 'normal' heterosexual couplings which concentrate on sexual activities in the early stages and then either break up or gradually place more emphasis on other kinds of jointly enjoyed pursuits. Nevertheless, the logic of the Bat-Ada argument is that permissive attitudes to recreational sex lead to a desire for more unusual forms, progress to increased prostitution and pornography and, among other forms of perversion, to more instances of sexual contact between adults and children. The scale of the problem is often claimed to be large and increasing, and reliable witnesses are found to assert this. For instance, in testimony before the Committee on the Judiciary of the United States Senate in November 1981, Ernest E. Allen, Chairman of the Jefferson County Task Force on Child Prostitution and Pornography, stated that he was 'convinced that there is indeed a national epidemic' (Allen 1981). The medical metaphor naturally leads to the notion that the disease of sexual permissiveness is contagious. Moreover the argument continues that this leads to the development of profitable and powerful 'industries' in child prostitution and pornography: to 'baby pros' and 'kiddie porn' as they are known in the United States (Heid Bracey 1979; Bridge 1978).

North American society seems particularly adept at developing a vivid language for this type of debate. A man who selects a boy partner for sexual relations and pays for the privilege is called a 'chickenhawk' (Lloyd 1979, p. 35). A three-year investigation into the sexual exploitation of children is referred to as the 'meat rack report' (Campagna 1985). The word 'sexploitation' has been coined to describe the set of phenomena associated with child sexual exploitation. As the problem and its vocabulary increase, so public awareness of the sexual exploitation of children and its commercial possibilities grows. Sometimes it is argued that this is a new phenomenon which is due to the breakdown of old values; at other times it is suggested that, because there is now social acceptance of the existence of a problem, cases which would once have been repressed are now brought to the light of public inquiry. A great deal of concern has recently been expressed in the United States about the revelation of sexual abuse practices in pre-school education. One such case involved the arraignment of seven people from the McMartin nursery school in Manhattan Beach, California on 208 charges of child molesting. The offences were allegedly associated with the production of pornographic material which was distributed through a vice ring. One result was that, in 1984, the state of California passed an 11.25 million dollar bill to expand anti-sex-abuse programmes in state schools. Another was that male teachers have been sacked and banned from employment in pre-school education throughout the United States. It also seems that concern about the sexual abuse of children has reached such a pitch that many adults are now wary of any physical contact with children (*Time,* 12 November 1984 pp. 91–2; personal communications, Jill E. Korbin).

Yet the picture is not entirely clear. As argued above, there is no logical progression from increased heterosexual activity either to satiation or to a search for abnormal sexual gratification, however one chooses to define 'abnormal'. And it could be claimed that the use of terms like 'kiddie porn' and 'meat rack' is sensationalist and prurient. Is it not denigration to refer to children as 'kids', comparing them with young animals, just as women are referred to as 'chicks' in pornographic literature? Could it not be argued that to refer to sexually exploited children as 'meat' is to think of them in the same way as do exploiters who treat them as objects?

Similar doubts may be cast on the many claims that the problem of sexual exploitation of children is increasing. If the equation permissiveness = satiation = perversion is true, then logically this exploitation will increase. Surely there must be some truth in this if responsible witnesses make confident claims to the United States Senate that the problem has reached epidemic proportions? Yet even the best estimates of the numbers of juvenile prostitutes may have poor statistical foundation. Nevertheless, because they are the only figures available, they enter official records and thus become facts, which may be quoted confidently by anyone. One example of this is the figure of one million child prostitutes in the United States, which was given in evidence to the House of Representatives in 1977. The expert in question was Dr Judianne Densen-Gerber, Director of the Odyssey Institute which operates rehabilitation programmes for children with various kinds of deviancy problem. The figure is a guestimate based on the number of 300,000 boy prostitutes given in what Dr Densen-Gerber refers to as 'the research of Robin Lloyd'. Because she assumed that there would indubitably be more girl prostitutes, she added 600,000 to this figure without providing any evidence to support her claim. Indeed, historical evidence about man–boy sexual preferences, and some figures given by other authorities in other countries, might contradict her assumption. But the real problem is that Lloyd is not a social scientist working on any kind of established methodology for gathering statistical information, but a journalist researching a book for the popular market. Here is his own account of how he arrived at the figure Dr Densen-Gerber quoted:

> In the early stages of research for this book, I approached police officers and leaders of the gay community with a working figure of 300,000 boy prostitutes in the United States alone. Deputy District Attorney James Grodin, in Los Angeles said, 'You won't get any argument from this office for that figure'. During a television interview I offered the same figure to Morris Kight, the West Coast gay activist. Said Kight, 'It might well be double that amount'.
>
> But what Kight and Grodin were agreeing to was – at its best – a gut hunch. (Lloyd 1979, p. 202)

None of these experts ever consider the alternative premise that the figure 'might well be' considerably less. I find this more than a little illogical, but then I am not impressed by the logic of the equation permissiveness = satiation = perversion.

It seems that in the field of sociosexual problems, the witness bears no burden of proof about the truth of statements, but is able to make a priori claims about the existence and extent of a set of facts which people in general find desperately uncomfortable. The nature of the evidence is such that research in this area could lead one to contradictory conclusions. Either the sexual exploitation of children is impossible and unthinkable and therefore does not exist (the repression effect), or it is a perpetual threat to every individual from birth to majority (the exaggeration effect). Exaggeration is often a characteristic of moral campaigns, which may combine assertions of increased immorality with assumptions about the inherent nature of human beings as evil, or of sexual impulses as uncontrollable except by strong will and external government. But human nature has not always been conceptualized in the same way. Different societies and historical epochs have different theories on the subject and there is no 'given' natural human state from which to argue. It is interesting to examine the ways in which different conceptualizations have been, and are being, used to justify various ways of behaving. There are similarities in behaviour, if not in concepts and beliefs, between moral campaigns in the twentieth century and the persecution of witches and satanists in earlier times, particularly because witch hunters so often used sexual imagery and might accuse their victims of having intercourse with satanic beings. An excellent example is Aldous Huxley's recreation of the exorcism of the Devils, who posessed a small priory of nuns in Loudun in seventeenth-century France, which shows how contemporary theories of both divine and human nature led inevitably to behaviour which would now be regarded as not only cruel but also ridiculous. The universal relevance of this for Huxley is that those involved in moral campaigns should be wary of paying more attention to evil than to good. By doing so they 'never succeed in making the world better, but leave it either as it was, or sometimes even perceptibly worse than it was, before the crusade began. By thinking primarily of evil we tend, however excellent our intentions, to create occasions for evil to manifest itself' (Huxley 1971 p. 175).

Although there has been no international crusade against child sexual exploitation on the scale noted in the United States and United Kingdom, the picture is drawn in much the same way on the international scene. In a report on child labour to the United Nations Sub-Commission on Prevention of Discrimination and Protection of Minorities, the Special

Rapporteur Abdelwahab Boudhiba (1982, p. 21) stated that 'There has always been a demand for children for sexual purposes because of their freshness and simplicity. Our age, which is 'permissive' and at the same time surfeited and sexually vulgarised in the extreme, seeks all kinds of erotic refinements . . . to renew . . . jaded sensuality'. He refers to a report by the children's charity SOS Enfants that there are 5,000 male and 3,000 female prostitutes under the age of 18 working in Paris; says that in Latin America clients prefer children aged 10–14; and that in Bangkok 'girls scarcely weaned are handed over to pimps'. This information is not supported by reference to any research or investigation. It is allied to the idea that there is a 'network of organized vice' involved in a traffic in actual children for sexual purposes and also of child pornography. Prostitution, as one Asian magazine puts it, 'is no longer just an affair private and local. It has become public and transnational, a blatant rape of a people' (*Balai* Vol. 11, No. 4, pp. 21–2). The result, according to many reports, is a profitable and powerful international industry. When children are not actually sold across national borders, tourists travel to use them on specially arranged sex tours. 'Top Firm Offers Naughty Tours to the City of Sin', announced a headline in the *Sunday People* (31 March 1985, pp. 12–13) discussing a trip to Bangkok, a capital city which *Time* magazine has called 'Lust City in the Far East' (10 May 1982 p. 27).

These issues are frequently discussed in all kinds of media outlets as well as in academic journals which relate the themes to debates about sexual freedom, childhood, feminism and human rights (e.g. Bridge 1978; Dudar 1977; Barry 1984; Finkelhor 1979). These are linked with tendencies in well-known, and easily available magazines like *Playboy* and *Penthouse*, which are sold under the category 'leisure' or 'recreation' in family bookstores and newsagents. Judith Bat-Ada claims that these magazines illustrate a general social acknowledgement in Western society of the commercial importance of child sexuality. The new '*Playboy* family', she suggests, consists of 'a sexually exploitative father; a dehumanised ridiculed mother; and a sexually precocious and eroticised child' (Lederer 1980).

Not all indications point to the relatively cosy, family sexuality of *Playboy* magazine. The apparent precocity of a group of young girls has been exploited with effect in the cinema over the past decade. Tatum O'Neal, Jodie Foster, Nastassja Kinski and Brooke Shields are among the better known examples. It is worth noting that Brooke Shields has been involved in legal action to prevent the publication of nude photographs taken of her while she was in her early teens. Moreover, Jodie Foster's sexuality may have been used cynically in the first instance. The part of the New York prostitute in the film *Taxi Driver*, for which she became famous, was originally written for an adult (Wapshott 1984; Frank 1977). Times have changed since the 1930s when Graham Greene suggested that child actress Shirley Temple was being exploited for her sexuality and found himself being sued for libel.

At the present time the sexual exploitation of children is constructed in Western and Westernized societies along several axes, which are independent of moral or social issues about child sexuality itself. The problem is related to general debates about sexual morality, particularly those concerning recreational rather than procreational sex, to ideas about powerful networks of international vice, and to the ways in which people think about childhood sexuality. The chapters of this book will examine the evidence, such as it is, about child prostitution and pornography and place it in the various social contexts in which these occur. It is my contention that what actually happens when children are sexually exploited or abused is frequently obscured by sensational accounts of the problem – by the repetition of shocking and poorly documented facts which reproduce the logic of the equation permissiveness = satiation = perversion. In order to avoid this approach, I shall examine not simply physical acts and biological facts, but also social structures. However it is experienced, childhood sexuality is caught up in two sets of power relations. These are the social dominations of male over female, and of elders over juniors. But the situation cannot simply be explained in terms of gender and age hierarchies. It is also entangled in class and race relations. A child's dependence and need for protection are not entirely attributable to biologically determined 'innocence' and weakness, but arise from the power relations which render him or her liable to exploitation, and which differ according to the age, race, class and gender both of the exploited and the exploiter.

Figure 1 is a graphic depiction of this statement, which shows the way in which different forms of exploitation interact. Thus a poor black boy has more power than a poor black girl, but can be oppressed by a rich black woman and even more so by a rich white woman. The two poles of the system are the overall power of rich white men and the overwhelming helplessness of poor black girls.

It is because this interaction of hierarchies is important to understanding the dimensions of child sexual exploitation that this book follows the procedure of examining first the contexts in which this abuse of human rights occurs. Publications and reports about the sexual exploitation of children usually begin (and often also end) by cataloguing cases and instances, without even stopping to explain exactly why these are exploitative. They also frequently confuse sexual exploitation with sexual abuse. The boundary between the two is not clear-cut, and the causal mechanisms of each within society are similar, but this book will not be dealing in detail with the sexual abuse of children except where the child's sexuality has become a commodity – principally in prostitution and pornography. There is ample and expert literature on the subject of incest and sexual abuse by both known individuals and strangers. What I am setting out to do is to open a professional debate on the sexual abuse of children by customers.

Despite this distinction, it is necessary to discuss the general themes of child sexuality, child rights, family and childhood before proceeding to examine the often patchy existing evidence about child sexual exploitation. In doing so

I hope to examine some of the stereotypes and myths about adult customers for child sexuality and to demonstrate that this exploitation is an integral part of the way in which we think about children, as well as of the systems of power into which we are all born.

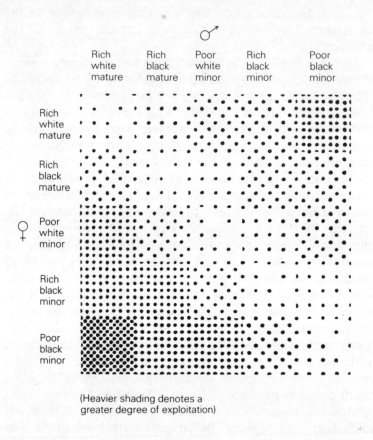

(Heavier shading denotes a
greater degree of exploitation)

Figure 1 The Dimensions of Exploitation.
Note: This graphic depiction of the relationship between age, gender, class and race shows exploitation shading the female half of the square most heavily. Equal relations may be thought of as possible between persons of the same age, sex, class and race, if personality factors are not taken into account.

1

The Sexually Innocent Child

So that's why it's funny of Mummy and Dad
This asking and asking in case I was bad.
A. A. Milne, *The Good Little Girl*

The idea that children are or should be sexually innocent is incorporated into ideas of childhood in general. Like all conceptualizations of social status, class or category, childhood has a changing historical and ethnographic appearance. In Western society it also seems to have a built-in ambiguity with constant interplay between ideas of good and evil and paradoxical attitudes towards sexuality. A relatively modern example of this interplay can be seen in children's literature and the media in the 1930s. This was the era in which Sigmund Freud's theories of infant sexuality began to be generally accepted in both medical circles and public ideology. Yet images of the sexually innocent child abounded and may have even increased. A. A. Milne's creation of the persona of Christopher Robin around the actual person of his own son Christopher is sometimes referred to in this context. Christopher Robin has the archetypical innocent childhood, whiled away in complete isolation from adults in the Hundred Acre Wood, accompanied by sexless woolly animals who are all of the male gender apart from the mother figure Kanga. Childhood ends when Christopher Robin goes away to school and adult life leaving his puzzled companions in the enchanted place at the end of *The House at Pooh Corner*. But until then he is unquestioned ruler of his own world. This middle-class, insulated nursery world was contemporary with the era of a particular genre of child stars in the cinema. The innocent purity of little Shirley Temple converted hard-bitten gamblers, thieves and tramps in film after film. Parents who would have been horrified at the thought of their own child walking off with a small hand trustingly placed in that of a dubious stranger were entranced by this charming picture of childhood. The curly-headed, self-confident Miss Temple became the model for a whole generation of little girls.

Nevertheless a further paradox is the rigidity with which the boundaries of the enchanted wood had to be drawn. Childcare manuals before the Second World War tended to instruct mothers in the importance of a 'properly planned routine', advocating 'early sphincter control, strict scheduling, early suppers and bedtimes for their salutary nature and for their utility in character and habit training' (Pottishman Wiess 1979, p. 32). The routines advocated by the childcare expert of the time, Truby King, were among the first to be applied to all classes, and placed the burden of correct child behaviour on the mother's correct observance of militarily precise routines (Comer 1979, p. 151). Children's good behaviour was a measure of parental good behaviour and children were constrained to obey adult rules regardless of any apparent absurdity. Many children must have agreed with Robert Louis Stevenson's complaint:

> In winter I get up at night
> And dress by yellow candlelight
> In summer quite the other way
> I have to go to bed by day.
> (*A Child's Garden of Verses*)

When a child is born it is not just introduced to a world of light and air with which it copes according to its biological capacities, from the confusion of which it will learn to perceive sights and sounds, and within which it will move and grow. It is also born into a social position. Although genetic inheritance may be important, particularly in the case of mental or physical handicap, the social world has already predetermined many import factors in the child's access to and enjoyment of the physical world. Class, race and creed as well as family structure play their parts in preparing a place for the child in ways that are not given by the physical world. But, in all cases, the status of child is immutable. All individuals are affected by this for a longer or shorter period of their lives.

Few social scientists have made a serious study of childhood. Most attempts tend to agree with the anthropologist Margaret Mead that human universals of childhood can be sought through cross-cultural comparison, because there are recurrent biological similarities in growth, in parent–child relationships and in the needs of children. For Mead, one universal similarity is that adults regard children as weak, helpless and in need of protection, supervision and training (Mead 1955, p. 7). She claims that there are three cross-cultural variations on the theme of mother–child relationships, and it is important to note that she does not mention fathers. 'To the extent that the child's whole individuality is emphasised, there is symmetry; to the extent that its weakness and helplessness are emphasised there is complementary behaviour; and to the extent that the mother gives not only her breast, but milk, there is the beginning of reciprocity' (Mead 1962, p. 78).

Some historians, on the other hand, have provided evidence that protected childhood is a relatively modern conception. According to writers like Ariès, Plumb, de Mause and Hunt, prior to the fifteenth century European children were considered to be adults with corresponding rights and responsibilities by the time they reached the age of six or seven years (Ariès 1973, Plumb 1972, de Mause 1979, Hunt 1970). The word 'child' implied only kinship and status and did not refer to an age hierarchy. Many pictorial records of the time show children depicted as miniature adults engaged in adult activities. But these were the sons and daughters of the nobility. Painters depicted their own children in charming, domestic portraits which reveal that children were not always viewed as small adults. Even though the dominant ideology suppressed childhood and used children as pawns in economic and political alliances, a space did exist for the type of childhood which would be recognizable in the twentieth century (Fuller 1979, pp. 80–1).

Christianity and Christian ideology have always held

children up as exemplars for living. Becoming 'like little children' is a condition of entering the kingdom of heaven and this has ensured that childhood has been accorded a special conceptual status throughout the Christian era. Religious painting swarms with cherubs, and the Holy Family is always constructed around the central figure of the Christ Child. But, prior to the seventeenth century, adults and children were both taken to be existing in a state of original sin, in which both old and young stood in equal danger of hell. The moral separation of child and adult occurred at the same time as the rise of new educational practices, which were encouraged by the ideas of orders like the Jesuits and also by Romanticism. Instead of sharing the state of original sin with adults, children were believed to be born in a state of innocence, in which they needed protection from corruption by adult society. Among the upper and middle classes at least, childhood became a period of 'quarantine' during which special separate, protective treatment was necessary. As Ariès puts it, 'the solicitude of family, church, moralists and administrative administrators deprived the child of the freedom he had hitherto enjoyed among adults' (Ariès 1973, p. 397).

This change of moral status for children coincided with changes in religion itself. The rise of Protestantism was not only contemporary with the rise of new classes in society, which required particular forms of education for their children, it also coincided with the development of the modern family form, based on conjugal units. In religion, the moral aspect gradually superceded the sacred. The cult of the Infant Jesus, symbolizing childhood innocence, dates from this time. Increased attention to the Holy Childhood as a model for all childhoods provided a rationale for the maintenance of conjugal units for protecting the innocence of the products of marriage. Although real families seldom did or do conform to a nuclear pattern, the idea that a nurturing married couple is the best unit for raising children became a moral imperative.

Through the social acceptance of this concept of childhood, new ideas of the family were organized around the central personage of the child (Meyer 1977; Ariès 1973, p. 396). These permeated working-class life through the intervention of state agencies and experts. The healthy family was circumscribed by law as having specific functions and performances and taking the correct nuclear form (Meyer 1977; Donzelot 1980). The child was the state's hostage in the centre of the family. Its welfare and need for protection have come to provide a rationale for state intervention; dismantling unsuccessful families on the one hand and providing child benefit payments on the other. Childhood in Western societies has become a problem area which is too difficult for parents to deal with. Experts in a range of new sciences like pediatrics, psychology and psychoanalysis provide the solutions to the problems and disseminate them in a mass of popular literature (Donzelot 1980, p. 395).

Yet as the Victorians uncovered the special life of childhood they also revealed childhood sexuality. Children were described as 'little angels' and 'closer to God' than other mortals. Like women they were 'purer' than adult males, and the ideas of femininity and childhood were and are interrelated myths. But children's ideologically asexual appearance was always threatened with denial by a barely suppressed acknowledgement of their actual sexuality. Thus women also had to be protected and controlled or they would 'fall' and become 'bad' – an idea with a further echo of biblical mythology. The Victorian fascination with and repression of sexuality in all its forms is too well catalogued to need discussion here. It is a necessary corollary of the assertion of childhood innocence because this assertion implicitly acknowledges the existence of sexuality in children and adolescents. To take up Jane's complaint in the A. A. Milne verse which heads this chapter, why is it necessary to constantly ask an axiomatically innocent child if it has been good? If children and young people are sexually innocent, why do adults prevent attempts at masturbation and separate the sexes in schools? As Michel Foucault points out in his *History of Sexuality*, such actions are statements that childhood sexuality exists and that it is a public problem which becomes the concern of doctors, teachers and parents, and the rationale for the development of innumerable institutions and discursive practices (Foucault 1979). The cult of innocence developed and strengthened towards the end of the last century, possibly as a defence against advances in the awareness of the sexual life of children represented in theories like those of Sigmund Freud. The cocoon of protection which segregates children from adults would not be necessary if children were indeed absolutely innocent and ignorant of sex (Fuller 1979, p. 6).

Changes in attitude towards children also had an economic basis. Through a combination of philanthropic and trades union campaigning, children were banned from the workforce during the course of the nineteenth century. At the turn of the century, child labour reforms had been so effective that work had become part of the conceptualization of male adulthood, and play essentially linked with ideas of childhood. Work refers of course to paid employment. Women's work became housework and children's work was transformed into schooling. Educational reforms had provided compulsory institutions which supervised both socialization and training for the labour force. Further institutions, like social work and juvenile courts, which are specific to childhood, had appeared during a period of intense philanthropic activism which one historian has dubbed the 'child saving era' (Platt 1969). The prevailing mood in the early part of the twentieth century was summed up thus by one woman writer:

> It is the vision of all children, as the assets of the race, to be conserved at any cost – as the torch bearers of the civilization of the future, as the links in the chain of human endeavor. With this vision before mankind, the child has in our own day entered into his [sic] rights. For the first time in the history of the race, he has become an entity in himself: his physical needs, his mental requirements, his moral training as considerations to be studied

entirely apart from adults. His life has become an autonomous world set within that of maternity. (Simeral 1916, p. 7)

Childcare ideas have changed in the twentieth century from the strict regimes of Truby King. After the end of the Second World War a close mother–child bond was believed to be important and the dangers of maternal deprivation were used to justify the exclusion of mothers from the workforce. The chief exponent of this theoretical position was John Bowlby, whose ideas influenced the United Kingdom government's development of the welfare state and were also used by the World Health Organization. The contrast with Truby King's separatist attitude is marked:

> A child needs to feel he [*sic*] is an object of pleasure and pride to his mother; a mother needs to feel an expansion of her own personality in the personality of her child: each needs to feel closely identified with the other. The mothering of a child is not something which can be arranged by rota, . . . possible . . . only if the relationship is continuous. (Bowlby 1965, p. 77)

The theories of Dr Benjamin Spock allowed a more liberal approach to child rearing. More recently there has been a tendency to common-sense theories and the book market has been flooded by a series of manuals written or ghost-written by non-expert personalities known through their activities in other fields. These apparently urge parents to use their own innate wisdom in their approach to their offspring. This does not result in a greater sense of freedom for either parent or child but, as one observer puts it, 'the common sense rules represent the lowest common denominator of everyday childcare and practice' resulting in 'a high degree of consensus on what's best for children' (Comer 1979, p. 153).

The modern form of childhood has two major aspects. The first is a rigid age hierarchy which permeates the whole of society and creates a distance between adults and children. The status difference is enhanced by special dress, special games, special artefacts (toys), special language and stories, which are all considered appropriate to what Ariès calls the 'quarantine' period of childhood. The distance is further enhanced by the second aspect, which is the myth of childhood as a 'golden age'. Happiness is now the key term associated with innocence – childhood must be a happy time as well as a time of separation from corrupt adult society. Parental obligation consists in providing this happiness by centring the family on the child. The child becomes an object of attention and love, expressed as often as not in the provision of consumer goods by the parents and their rapid consumption by children. In the late twentieth century Jane would be more likely to be asked 'have you enjoyed yourself?' than 'have you been good?'. Both parent and child can be enmeshed in guilt as a result. Children are now obliged to be happy, just as they were formerly obliged to be good. Parents have failed if their children manifest lack of enjoyment, just as they used to be blamed if their children showed bad behaviour. Yet the feminist writer Shulamith Firestone suggests:

> It is clear that the myth of childhood happiness flourishes so wildly not because it satisfies the needs of children but because it satisfies the needs of adults. In a culture of alienated people, the belief that everyone has at least one good period in life, free of care and drudgery dies hard. And obviously you can't expect it in your old age. So it must be you've already had it. This accounts for the fog of sentimentality surrounding any discussion of childhood or children. Everyone is living out some private dream on their behalf. (Firestone 1971, p. 93)

This type of conceptualization of childhood has dominated Western family law and family life throughout the twentieth century. It was codified by Eglantyne Jebb when she started the Save the Children movement in 1919 and thus passed into what has become known as the international community. For this century has seen the rise of a further phenomenon: the idea that 'how a sovereign state treats its own citizens is no longer a matter for its own exclusive determination, but a matter of *legitimate* concern for all other states, and for their inhabitants' (Sieghart 1985, p. vii). Human Rights Law is now universal and independent of any particular culture or ideology, and the special needs of children are acknowledged in many declarations, covenants and charters.

In 1945 the United Nations Charter established the existence of an international community which has the respect of human rights and fundamental freedoms as one of its objects. Children are mentioned in the Universal Declaration of Human Rights, which was adopted by the United Nations in 1948: 'Motherhood and childhood are entitled to special care and assistance. All children, whether born in or out of wedlock, shall enjoy the same social protection' (Article 25, paragraph 2). They are assured of similar protective measures under Article 24 of the International Covenant on Civil and Political Rights which is signed by 80 nations and came into force in 1976. Paragraphs in Articles 10 and 12 of the International Covenant on Economic, Social and Cultural Rights, which was signed by 77 nations in the same year, agree upon further protective measures. Not least among these international pronouncements is the Declaration of the Rights of the Child, which is based on Eglantyne Jebb's precepts, and became a Resolution of the United Nations General Assembly in 1959. Article 9 is the most relevant to a discussion of sexual exploitation. It states that

> the child shall be protected against all forms of neglect, cruelty and exploitation. He [*sic*] shall not be the subject of traffic in any form. The child shall not be admitted to employment before an appropriate minimum age; he shall in no case be caused or permitted to engage in any occupation or employment which would prejudice his health or education, or interfere with his physical, mental or moral development.

None of these instruments refer explicitly to a child's sexuality or imply anything other than protection as the right of a child. As we shall see in chapter 3, there have recently been changes in attitude towards children's rights and the 1979 UN Year of the Child resulted in one initiative among non-governmental organizations to draft a Convention of the Rights of the Child, which also includes the notion of enabling rights and the child's need for a degree of autonomy. Yet the prevailing norms of childhood still entail innocence and protection, not only in the West, but also among influential intergovernmental organizations.

Two sets of ideas thus define the notions of childhood current in the international community, and these are based on Western precepts. The first separates children from adults, defining the ideal family as a nuclear unit consisting of protected children and protecting adults. The maintenance of family form and the state of childhood is ensured through the existence of bodies of knowledge and groups of experts, who advise on the socially defined problems of the adult–child relationship and act in order to eradicate or alter irregular situations. The second set of ideas separates adults from children within the production process. The child cannot be a worker, at least not within the formal labour force. Because it is a child, it needs to be protected and it must be excluded from the workplace with its economic dependence ensured. The exclusion of women is, or has been, effected by the same means, for the justification for this exclusion is protecting children by keeping them at home with their own mothers. Nevertheless, children are also regarded as needing a special kind of socialization which cannot be provided within the family group. Education serves a double purpose. It teaches the skills and habits required by the formal economy, while operating a process of selection and rejection which reproduces the system of stratification. At the same time it provides an additional form of control of childhood which is external to the private family world. The fact that the domestic group does not lend itself to easy external regulation accounts for the necessity for strong ideological controls in state socialization apparatuses, and accounts for the overdevelopment of conventional family and sexual norms in the content of school curricula.

Ideas of childhood and parenthood are also exported from the West, often using the mechanisms of international agencies, and are frequently utilized as control mechanisms. The idea of childhood as a period of lack of responsibility, with rights to protection and training but not to autonomy, may be culturally irrelevant in countries where a high proportion of children work alongside adults from an early age, or leave home to seek waged work from the age of eight or ten years old. But these ideas are used to promote the notion that correct parenthood consists of nuclear family structures with particular methods of contraception and patterns of consumption. These are not only disseminated through the official discourse of national agencies or international bodies like UNICEF. The stereotypes also permeate the mass media, as I have observed during fieldwork in several different countries.

When a Peruvian mother and father who live in one bare room with their several children pick up a daily newspaper, they are likely to read articles with titles like 'Make your Child's Room into a Place Where he can Discover Himself' ('Haga el cuarto del nino un lugar donde mande el' (*El Observador* Lima, 1 June 1982). This not only casts doubt on the type of parenting they are able to provide, but also draws attention to their poverty because they are unable to provide a separate room for every child. But in addition it draws attention to their racial characteristics, because such articles are typically accompanied by a photograph of a blond, blue-eyed Western child – the ideal of happiness which Shulamith Firestone describes as 'as blonde and beefy as a Kodak advertisement' (Firestone 1971, p. 91).

Mass media entertainment often contains the same messages about correct childhood. One of the most popular forms of family entertainment in Latin America in the early 1980s was provided by a group of child singers, whose activities were depicted in films imported from Spain. The minimal plots of these films focus on aspects of the generation gap, portraying war between children and stereotypical aggravating adults, like teachers. The members of the group, which is called Parchis, are children whose existence seems to consist of play, pranks, fashionable clothes, attractive homes and songs on sweetly innocent themes. They are also all Caucasian. Because they seem to be living a trouble-free lifestyle they can only reinforce feelings of lack of worth and self-denigration among dark-skinned, brown-eyed, poor children who idealize not only the values but also the appearance of these 'happy' children.

The tendency towards self-deprecation among poor, 'Indian' children in Peru is further reinforced in educational texts. Civic education includes socialization into the rights and duties of family members but, in the official text books, the family is depicted as nuclear in form, Caucasian in appearance and containing only two children. The results of this were clear to me when I was researching child workers in Lima. I was collecting essays on out-of-school activities and often asked children who finished the task quickly to draw a picture in the time available. One of the titles I gave them was 'My Family'. Almost without exception, they reproduced the Western style family of the textbooks, many of them carefully tracing the pictures from their schoolbooks. When I asked them about their own families it was clear that many included a large number of children, and that many were step-parent or single-parent units. Few lived in nuclear families and none were Caucasian. These results were not only the result of authoritarian styles of teaching which repress individual response. For these children, many of whom were as young as five or six years old, their own families were not legitimate entities – their own experience of domestic life was invalidated by the 'correct' stereotype.

Third World children have a contrasting image in European mass media. Starving, ragged children stare out of news stories and advertisements for development charities. Even if the projects for which money is sought are not directly related to children, children are frequently used to make the appeal; thus an association is constantly made between white children who have a correct childhood and black children who have none.

The process continues in the marketing of commodities. As in the West, advertisements which are directed at the child market show products enshrined in the false image of an intact and happy world, which repeat to children and parents that happiness and love depend upon receiving the advertised commodity from parents. It also begins a life-long association between feeling good and consuming (Pestalozzi 1981). These images are most frequently received by the poor through the medium of television, for even the poorest shack in a shanty town, lacking water and sewage, may still have an illegal electricity supply and a television set. The images which flicker in the windowless huts are almost universally drawn from Western contexts or from the indigenous Western-influenced middle class. This happiness is unobtainable, yet it may be the only available knowledge of life outside the slum. The sense of cultural deprivation and lack of personal worth is reinforced by the information that they are failing even in the basic roles of parents and children. What is more, because the television programmes sold by the West to developing countries depict Western middle-class or fantasy existence, as in *Dallas* and *Dynasty*, slum dwellers are unlikely to find out about the existence of poverty or even of a working class in the West. This increases the isolation of the poor and leads to a sense of national failure which adds to the crushing weight of personal failure. In this way childhood becomes a valuable commodity in the power structure of relationships between developed and developing nations.

2

The Sexually Knowing Child

Younger than she are happy mothers made.
Shakespeare, *Romeo and Juliet*

There are observable physiological criteria which provide good reasons for distinguishing adults from children. For that matter, there are clearly observable stages within childhood itself. Although age can be used as a criterion, it is simplest to think of three broad stages through which all children pass: infancy (0–5 years), pre-pubertal childhood (6–12 years) and post-pubertal adolescence (12 years to adulthood or the age of political majority). Adolescence, like childhood, has been claimed to be a relatively recent social invention. Like childhood, Western adolescence is regarded as a 'special' era, with its own needs, problems, artefacts, economics and language. Adults are shut out of adolescent life through the ideology of the 'generation gap'. This assures them that they will not have the same tastes and views as their 'teenage' children, that adolescents will have secrets from them, and that there are specific problems such as drugs, sex and delinquency to which their adolescent offspring are prone and which, if they appear, are further evidence of incorrect parenting.

Throughout the three stages there are notable differences in physical capacities, linguistic and reasoning abilities and sexual development. The difference between infant and adult is the most marked. The dividing lines between infant/child, child/adolescent and adolescent/adult are usually blurred, and vary according to sex, class and culture.

In infancy, the need for shelter, nurture and protection is most marked. Infants and toddlers are incapable of most of the movements and tasks which adults enjoy. Their physical strength is markedly less and they have little capacity for self-defence and independent existence. They develop from having no language to the acquisition of a limited linguistic competence and their reasoning is pre-logical. But despite the cult of the innocent babe, many authorities claim that these small individuals do have a strong autoerotic sensuality and that sexuality in this stage is vitally important because of the effects it has on future adult personality. Sensory pleasure is gained by infants from actions like sucking, defecation and micturition as well as overall skin stimulation and genital touching. Nevertheless, while this gratification may be hedonistic and sensual, the child gives it no social meaning until it receives information from adult attitudes, language and prohibitions.

Socially and psychosexually the influence of sex characteristics and related gender attributes are of crucial importance from birth. From the moment when the midwife announces 'it's a girl' or 'it's a boy', biological differences are used to distinguish female from male. But social life also constructs systems of gender which assign feminine and masculine attributes on the basis of physiological differences. The relatively simple anatomical differences between female and male are taken as the starting point for some of the most basic social structural distinctions in human society. As if the anatomical differences were not sufficiently striking in themselves, many societies provide systems of bodily markings which further differentiate either the sexual organs themselves, as in clitoridectemy and circumcision, or other parts of the body, in different customs of dressing hair as well as in tattooing and scarification. On top of this, gender systems determine acceptable male and female dress, behaviour and roles which often vary widely between different cultures and at different times. Who would have believed in England in 1945, for instance, that 40 years later a whole generation of males would wear an ear-ring in one ear in late puberty in order to give the appearance of adult masculinity?

The process of acquiring language is now regarded as having important effects on the development of a child's sexual identity: 'The small human animal is forced into society by the fact that a culture and language pre-exist the individual, and if the child is to put forward any demands, it must acquire language and therefore the positions of sexed identity – masculine and feminine – necessitated by that culture' (Coward 1978).

The meaning of human sexuality is socially constructed and changes dramatically across cultures and throughout history. Children not only find themselves placed within an age hierarchy but also, however young and however innocent, they are part of the division of society according to sex. And it is biologically determined sex, not socially defined gender, which really makes the difference in the last instance, because all gender systems take their justification from observed physiological distinctions and from the consequences these can have in adult life. Although the rules involved are external to individuals, they are not impersonal, for they affect the ways in which people think about themselves. In the course of development from infant to adult in any society, individuals learn the current social rules which determine the sexual behaviour of men and women in their culture. These form a system of meaning which is made up of language, symbols and both explicit and implicit rules about behaviour. The developing individual becomes aware of how he or she is viewed within the sex and gender structure by other people of both sexes, and this becomes fundamental to his or her development and ideas of identity. In Western society infants come to know their gender identity by messages implicit in the artefacts and trimmings of their childhood identity. There are colours and styles of clothes appropriate to infants and toddlers of each gender; toys and games suitable for girls and others for boys; stories for little girls and others for their brothers; even language and ways of touching boy and girl babies differ from the moment of birth. The interplay between age and gender in childhood is captured exactly by Peter Wollen in a brief discussion of children's toys:

It is important to realize that it is not only the difference in content which divides boys' toys from girls'; but also the difference in scale. In the same way that an adult is on a different scale to a child, so children are on a different scale to their toys. This difference of scale also embodies a difference of power. Children are able to exercise the same power over their toys as adults exercise over them.

But the contrast in scale is much greater for boys than for girls. Boys are typically in charge of whole armies or transportation systems or space projects, in which they manipulate large numbers of microscopic personnel. They are able to indulge fantasies of autocracy and omnipotence, which are the reverse of their destiny in life. Yet, at the same time, this ratio of superiority is preserved in the sexism and racism characteristic of our society . . .

Girls are offered narrower horizons and lesser scope for the exercise of power. Play for them is much more a kind of apprenticeship in which a consistent order is maintained through the transition from child to adult . . . they are promised the possibility of wielding authority over children of their own, instead of over dolls. (Wollen 1979, p. 54)

Through all these means, individuals enter the pre-pubertal childhood phase already knowing about some aspects of their sexuality. During this period, although their language skills and knowledge of the world are developing, both faculties are limited by children's rate of development and by the access which adults permit or encourage them to have to various aspects of culture. Until they reach early adolescence their ability to manipulate facts is, in any case, limited to concrete notions of causality. They may be aware of the facts of reproduction, for instance, in the sense of where babies come from ('Mummy's tummy') and even how they got there, though they may have gained this knowledge in different ways: observed actions, mechanical accounts or vague descriptions of loving acts. But they are unlikely to be able to comprehend the economic consequences of reproduction or the social consequences of irregular types of reproduction, let alone of irregular reproductive acts.

Nevertheless attitudes towards sex and sexual characteristics are rapidly assimilated. Cultural norms of shame are particularly easy to pass on to children through linguistic and bodily taboos. A group of six-year-old English boys will collapse into red-faced giggles if one of them utters the word 'bum' or may attempt to shock a female teacher with the use of more explicitly sexual words, without understanding the full implications of their meaning. Shame about hiding or revealing parts of the body varies widely between cultures and also age groups. Even in societies with strict rules of bodily modesty for adults, infants and young children may be permitted or encouraged to appear naked. And shame is not a prerogative of modernized societies, as some rearview-mirror theories of the noble savage would have us believe. Margaret Mead, who is usually remembered for her accounts of idyllic, sexual freedom in Samoa, provides the following description of sexual shame among the Manus of the Admiralty Islands to the north of what is now Papua New Guinea:

> Sex is conceived as something bad, inherently shameful, something to be relegated to the darkness of night. Great care is taken that the children should never be witnesses. In the one-room houses it is impossible to accomplish this, but the children soon learn the desirability of dissembling their knowledge. Their clandestine knowledge is as shamed, as marred by a sense of sin, as is their parents' indulgence. Children sleeping in another house will say formally to their host or hostess upon leaving a house, 'We slept last night, we saw and heard nothing'. (Mead 1942, pp. 126–7)

Children have greater physical size and mobility than infants and this can lead to independent involvement in activities outside the household group, which can vary from unsupervised street work in developing countries to ballet and riding lessons in the West. But in all cases their small size and strength relative to adults makes them vulnerable to adult violence, inside or outside the family group, and their lack of reasoning ability and political and social power leaves them vulnerable to manipulation by all older people. While developing sexual characteristics may fascinate some children, others may not be overtly interested without adult or peer group stimulation. Yet hetero-erotic activity within the peer group is reported to be common. Laurie Lee provides a picture of the mutual exploration between pre-pubertal children in the English countryside:

> They received me naturally, the boys and girls of my age, and together we entered the tricky wood. Daylight and an easy lack of shame illuminated our actions. Banks and brakes were our tiring-houses, and curiosity our first concern. We were awkward, convulsed, but never surreptitious, being protected by our long knowledge of each other. And we were all of that green age which could do no wrong, so unformed as yet and coldly innocent we did little more than mime the realities. (Lee 1962, p. 206)

All societies deal with the biological facts of sex through the social construction of ideas about sexuality. These are the rules which govern masculine and feminine characteristics, forms of attraction and courtship, mating and coupling, reproduction and family life. Children are of central importance in reproduction and family life – they are both the end result and starting point of sexual activity. The ways in which reproduction and child nurture are organized in domestic groups and households varies greatly between and within societies. Mating and coupling may take the form of life-long heterosexual monogamy, polygamy, serial monogamy, promiscuity and various types of homosexual unions. There are many variations in the actually occuring domestic groups which nurture, protect and socialize children, and any one individual may experience several of these at various times during a lifetime. There is no proof whatsoever that nuclear families are either the most common or the most successful form of child rearing. One strong-willed mother may provide more efficient and loving care than two weak-willed, warring parents. Nor is there any evidence to support ideas that pre-industrial extended family systems are more warm and loving than isolated nuclear units. Affectionate accounts of childhood in a 'family fug' such as that provided by Laurie Lee (Lee 1962, p. 66, for example) are contradicted by others which describe a 'close-knit suffocating little world of pain and suffering' as in the Russian childhood of Maxim Gorky (Gorky 1966, p. 25).

The most common systems under which non-adults are nurtured include:

Non family

1 Institutions like orphanages, boarding schools and reformatories.
2 Employers, particularly of domestic servants or apprentices.
3 Group cooperation in intentional communities like Kibbutzim and communes, or largely unintentional groups of special category persons as in the case of street children.
4 Non-reproductive households including homosexual couples, elderly people and groups of friends.
5 Fictive kinship groups and artificial families consisting of foster or adoptive parents and god-parents.

Family

6 Single-parent households, not always female, may be a stage in serial monogamy or in a so-called 'matrifocal' system in which fathers provide some support and visit for sexual services.
7 Three-generational, extended family headed by a heterosexual couple (or widow/widower) and including their male and/or female offspring, spouses and progeny.

8 Polygamous extended family consisting of a man
with more than one wife (polygyny) or a woman with
more than one husband (polyandry). May take a
three-generational form.

9 Nuclear family, consisting of a heterosexual couple
and their children.

10 Reconstituted or transitional nuclear family consisting of a heterosexual couple and some or all of
their children, with or without their children from
previous unions. Often only part of a cycle including
6 and 9.

11 Sibling and cousin groups, often formed as a result
of changes in types 7, 8 and 9.

There are only three possible types of biological kinship or
mating relationship: parent–child; spouse–spouse; brother–
sister. Yet human societies have found many ways of
combining these relationships and coping with the essential
facts, as well as the consequences, of sex and reproduction.
Moreover, this wide range of possibilities is observable not
only across cultures, but also within them. The practice of
polygamy is usually restricted to societies with particular
social and religious structures, although isolated cases occur
in other places. But in the course of research in Peru, I
encountered cases of all but types 3 and 8, and in the United
Kingdom all forms except 8, although 2 is rare. One is therefore tempted to ask what is meant by Article 16, paragraph 3
of the Universal Declaration of Human Rights which states
that 'The family is the natural and fundamental group unit of
society and is entitled to protection by society and the State.'

As in many international Charters and Declarations, this
paragraph about the family occurs in an Article which also
includes rights of people 'of full age' to marry. In other
words, in the view of internationally agreed conventions, the
formation of families is connected to ideas about marriage
and adult status. The recognition of the process of sexual
maturation is one of the vital markers of adult status. The
pre-pubertal child provides explicit evidence of difference

from a reproductively mature adult, because of the absence of secondary sexual characteristics like pubic hair. It is post-pubertal individuals who present a definitional problem for many societies: physically able to reproduce, they are yet regarded as needing measures of protection and control for both sexual and other purposes. Individuals of this age may be intellectually and linguistically able as well as physically powerful and sexually mature. Despite their intense visibility in many societies and the fact that they may be targetted economically as a consumer group, they are nevertheless economically and politically powerless. Adults also often have and exert bodily and sexual rights over this age group.

The key to understanding the context in which adolescent sexuality is experienced is not the well-publicized turbulence of physiolgial changes. Growth and change in adolescence is nowhere as marked or dramatic as they are in infancy. The important factor is adult power, which is manifested in a series of legal instruments which fix the age of majority. This is generally taken to be the age at which full citizen's rights are achieved, whatever these may be. It varies between different cultures, usually on a range between 16 and 25, and sometimes only applying to males. But it is related to a series of other instruments which define the end of childhood and the beginning of adult responsibility for various purposes and at different stages throughout adolescence.

Adolescence is not just an ambiguous area in the physical sense, it is also defined as contradictory by law. According to legislation, childhood is defined by chronological criteria, even though the critical ages vary. By fixing the age of majority and franchise, legislation defines childhood as a time without political responsibility which, at the same time, lacks political power. The end of childhood in this sense tends to occur at the end of adolescence, around the time of full physical maturity and economic independence. Until that time the child or minor has no right to choose the type of polity under which he or she lives. Paradoxically, in most countries males, and sometimes females, under this age are allowed, or even expected, to fight and perhaps die to defend that polity (Ennew 1985b). By fixing the ages of criminal responsibility, which may vary according to the infractions committed, childhood is defined as a time of legal innocence when norms and sanctions are not fully understood. By fixing the age for compulsory education and the minimum ages at which various types of work can be performed, childhood is defined as a time of play and socialization, rather than work and economic responsibility. In addition, the interplay between the age at which education ends and that at which work begins, which is determined to a large extent by class and gender factors, determines the position in the labour market of the child and future adult.

Legislation defines childhood along two sexual criteria. The first is the age of consent to sexual activities and the second is the age of marriage, with or without parental consent. The social acceptance of full sexual rights varies within wide limits and often reveals extreme contradictions. The history of English law on sexual consent provides a case in point. The age of consent for heterosexual acts was fixed at 16 in 1885. Before that time, heterosexual intercourse between an adult male and a girl, with her consent, was not illegal. Nineteenth-century scandals about child prostitution resulted in pressure to change the law, and it became a crime for an adult male to have sexual intercourse with a female under 16 years old, whether she had consented or not, and a worse offence if she was under 13. Yet, paradoxically, the age for marriage was not raised from 12 to 16 until 1929 (Honoré 1978, pp. 81–2). The law affecting homosexual relations is equally contradictory. A boy reaches the age of majority at 18 for all purposes except the right to consent to homosexual relations – for that he must wait until he is 21. Homosexual relations between females of whatever age remain unregulated by law. Similar variations occur throughout Europe (see figure 2).

Figure 2 Variations in Sexual Legislation in European Countries.

The Draft Convention of the Rights of the Child raises a new issue in the field of international legislation regarding children. It highlights the need to secure not only the child's established right to special protection, but also the more positive 'enabling' rights, which recognize a degree of self-determination. In the 1959 United Nations Declaration of the Rights of the Child the form taken by protection is clearly envisaged as the care of biological parents in family life (Principle 6). This assumption lies behind much, perhaps most, international and national legislation. The principle of *patria potestas* in the family law of most nations secures the autonomy of the family unit, together with the rights of parents to make decisions for the welfare of their offspring while they are minors. But, as child abuse studies in many countries have shown, living with parents does not always ensure the best physical and emotional development of children (Korbin 1981), nor does it exclude sexual abuse. Most children are abused in family situations.

Many legislations recognize the dangers of *patria potestas* by providing the state with powers to intervene in 'unsuccessful' families and possibly assume parental rights. The principle governing such intervention is the 'best interests of the child', which may conflict at times with parental interests. A choice usually has to be made between removing children altogether, or using state or voluntary agencies to support the family unit and maintain its continued existence (Hoelgaard 1984). A child's right to protection from abusing parents also entails modification of *patria potestas*, with the result that parental rights are balanced by parental obligations. In some cultural settings, where parental (particularly paternal) power is regarded as absolute and is the model for state power, the implementation of these changes in family law can only be brought about by programmes of public education which emphasize that parental right and filial duty must be balanced by child right and parental duty (Becerra 1985). This also entails realizing that parenthood is best regarded as a privilege, rather than as the right to have children, or a burden for which children must pay. By using this type of argument I am not trying to make out a case against the family, but rather against the misuse of parental power and the social oppression which adults often exercise over children. The social function of the family is to nurture rather than to dominate. Moreover it is essential to avoid complacent attitudes towards 'the family', which are often combined with preconceptions about the inevitable "failure" of families which are regarded as irregular because they do not conform to the nuclear family model.

3

The Sexual Rights of Children

In all legal theory and practice, rights and duties are symmetrical. It is a popular fallacy to believe that this symmetry applies within the same individual: that if I have a right, *I* must also have a correlative duty. This is not so: if I have a right, *someone else* must have a correlative duty; if I have a duty, *someone else* must have a corresponding right.

Paul Sieghart, *The Lawful Rights of Mankind*

The ideal of childhood innocence presumes that children's sexual rights consist of protection not only from sexual abuse and exploitation but also in some cases from knowledge of sexuality and the facts of reproduction. But because even childhood has different stages, the need for protection varies. It could also be argued that protection is only achieved by giving at least older children sufficient knowledge to be able to protect themselves. Articulate adolescents are liable to demand this knowledge and even younger children are likely to have already amassed a good deal of information through exploratory activities and observing the adult world. Legal debates about the right to protection also involve the question of whether a child can make informed decisions about sexual or other matters (Children's Legal Centre 1985). Perhaps it can be argued that adults have a duty to ensure that this information is not only adequate, to ensure protection, but also well-grounded in current moral and cultural norms.

As pointed out in the Introduction, moral absolutists tend to claim that norms should never be regarded as current – they are fixed according to specific universal codes of moral practice. In the Jewish-Christian codes which dominate

Western ideologies, the precepts which govern the sexual behaviour of young people are usually regarded as those which state that parents should be honoured and adultery should not be committed, to which is often added that killing is not permitted. Translated into socio-moral and legal ideas, honouring parents has become the law of *patria potestas*, which outlines parental and particularly paternal rights over children. Until quite recently in English law parents could evoke *habeus corpus* to recover custody of their children against their wishes and a now discredited ruling of the Court of Chancery 1883 (re: Agar-Ellis 24 ChD 317) held that paternal rights were paramount over maternal (Children's Legal Centre 1985). The moral interpretation of adultery, which concerns the behaviour of married people, is often confused with fornication and one of the consequences has been a cult of pre-marital chastity, particularly for women. Historically this had a relationship to inheritance of property and the importance of ensuing legitimacy, particularly for the middle classes, and largely constitutes male control over women's sexuality. Thus fathers, brothers and husbands have a right and a duty to protect and regulate the sexual activities of daughters, sisters and wives. The principle of legitimacy ensures that the crucial family functions of reproduction and socialization of children take place only within specific family structures governed by specific laws of matrimony and ideas of morality (Millet 1971, p. 33). Until recently European women (like children) were legal minors, ultimately dependent upon males. The ideology of female weakness, based on ideas of physical, intellectual and moral incapacities, legitimated this position. Women needed to be protected both from other men and from their own emotions. The ideology of this type of family relies upon the interplay of two forms of hierarchy: that in which male dominates female, and that in which older people dominate younger ones. Moreover as the historian Peter Laslett (1980, p. 7) has noted, in England at least: 'Rules of respectability – Western, white, Anglo-Saxon, Protestant, Victorian and post-Victorian, middle-class respectability above all – are much more drastic than the principle of legitimacy requires, and more restrictive than is laid down by the established law of the State and even by the demands of Christian conviction.'

The incidence of extra-marital births tends to be taken as an index of societal immorality. An illegitimate child is evidence of an unsanctioned sexual act or, to put it another way, a woman out of control. The birth of an illegitimate child to a sexual minor is an even greater scandal, for it breaches the rules of both fundamental family hierarchies. It is therefore not surprising that of all the dangers of adolescent sexual activity, the one to which most attention is paid is early pregnancy. There are medical as well as social reasons for this. Adolescent pregnancy leads to increased obstetric risk, and is associated with increased risk of premature birth, perinatal mortality and morbidity, child abuse and neglect (McIntish 1984). It also affects the future course of the young mother's life, disturbing her chances of continuing education in many cases.

When a child becomes pregnant this is usually regarded as the most unwelcome of all unwanted pregnancies. Preventative solutions range from chastity to contraception and abortion. This is where the question of the sexual rights of children becomes entangled in the precepts about honouring parents, not committing adultery and not killing. This was revealed in a recent legal controversy in the United Kingdom in which a 1984 Court of Appeal ruling (later overturned by the House of Lords) stated that contraceptive advice could not be given to a person under the age of 16 without parental consent. This ruling entailed the principle that parents have the absolute right to control the bodies and sexuality of their children until they reach 16, unless a court intervenes (Children's Legal Centre 1985). This particular court decision was the result of a private action brought by Mrs Victoria Gillick, a Roman Catholic mother, against the Department of Health and Social Security and her Health Authority, regarding the possibility that local Family Planning Clinics might provide contraceptive and/or abortion advice to her four daughters while they were under the age of sixteen, without her prior knowledge and irrefutable evidence of her consent. Because of Mrs Gillick's declared religious convictions, this case may be regarded as being concerned not only with 'parental responsibility and family stability', as she states, but also an interpretation given to the commandment against killing by her Church. Although Mrs Gillick's expressed intention was to prevent her daughters receiving contraceptive advice under the age of consent, the fact that she is a Roman Catholic might also imply that she would not wish advice on either mechanical means of contraception or abortion to be available to them or any other women of any age.

If the legal criteria for a person giving valid consent to an act is that the consent is 'informed', then removing a potential source of information from children effectively quarantines those under 16 from the adult world. In the wake of the 'Gillick Ruling', booksellers in some areas of the United Kingdom removed from sale two best-selling sex guidance books for young people. This was as a result of pressure from a group called 'The Family and Youth Concern Society' which described the books as 'subversive' and 'anti-parent', and stated that they 'brutalize sex for young people' by advising them to seek advice on contraception from doctors or Family Planning Clinics.

Yet even Mrs Gillick refers to parental responsibility rather than parental rights, implying that the parent–child relationship is not composed solely of a child's duty to honour its parents but entails also the parent's obligation to nurture the child. The main argument in children's rights is whether parental responsibility consists only of an obligation to protect or whether it also includes a measure of enablement, of helping children to become independent and capable of making informed, autonomous decisions.

Whether adults recognize the validity of their decisions or not, children are frequently involved in issues of enormous social and political importance, and not always in the role of victims or innocents in need of particular care and protection. Legal minors, many of whom have barely reached adolescence, have been in the forefront of anti-apartheid action in South Africa. Children take part in the political violence in Northern Ireland and fight and die in Iran, Uganda and Nicaragua. But this involvement in the adult world is not a recent event. The Children's Crusades of the Middle Ages mobilized thousands of children from eight years old and upwards to march hundreds of miles across Europe with the idea of recapturing the Holy Land for Christianity. The leaders were not adult exploiters but 12-year-old boys like Stephen of Cloyes (Gray 1871). In the same era, boys of that age recruited and led armies and were responsible for major state decisions.

One of the first attempts at achieving specific rights for children was a petition presented to Parliament in 1669 by a boy believed to be connected with the Levellers, a political party and sect associated with ideas of social equality and incipient feminism. The petition described itself as 'A Modest Remonstrance of that untolerable grivance our Youth lie under, in the accustomed Severities of the School-discipline of this Nation' (MSS in the British Museum, quoted in Hoyles ed. 1979, p. 214). Children's Rights have sometimes been associated with egalitarian ideals. After being exiled for his part in the Paris Commune, Jean Valles tried to found a league for the protection of the rights of children. Modern writers on the subject, like A. S. Neill, have often been involved in libertarian or anarchist traditions. Thus, despite the ideological importance of the cult of innocence and the associated creed of the special need of the child (and its mother) for protection, there has always been a thread of counter-argument which urges that the child is not a hostage of the state within the family, nor the property of its parents, but rather an individual citizen of the state, whose interests can be considered and whose rights can be advocated along-side those of any other citizen. Children now tend to be regarded in Western law, if not in social practice, as persons. They are no longer romanticized as 'angels', or controlled, exchanged and exploited as chattels. Yet their position in the twentieth century continues to be ambiguous. Changes in legal and social attitudes may have less to do with humanizing societies than with 'the increasing cost of children together with their decreasing economic utility' (Stier 1978, p. 54). Ambiguities are nowhere more likely to raise heated arguments than in the field of sexual rights because, as has been shown, changes in this area involve the basic principles of age and gender domination which underlie not only social and legal structures, but also cultural imperatives.

Despite the ambiguities, the overriding rationale for limiting children's access to adult sexual knowledge and practices is their protection. Leaving aside arguments about innocence and the asexuality of childhood, it is still possible to argue that children, like all other persons, have a right to be protected against the manipulation and exploitation of their sexuality. What exactly does manipulation and exploitation mean in this case? In many of the standard works on the subject it appears that any kind of sexual contact between an adult and a child is regarded as exploitative. Expert testimony to the US House of Representatives in 1978 defined sexual exploitation of children as including: 'Any act committed by an adult designed to stimulate a child sexually or any act in which the child is used for the sexual stimulation of an adult – either the perpetrator or another adult' (Swift 1978). This particular definition includes acts of touching as well as intercourse and 'psychological sexual exploitation', including threats of sexual acts and watching sexual acts. The term exploitation is more usually taken to have something to do with a third party, who profits from the use of labour in particular forms of servitude. This is the meaning in the International Covenant on Economic, Social and Cultural Rights – which is one of the major international instruments, with 80 countries as signatories. Article 10, paragraph 3 states that: 'Children and young persons should be protected from economic and social exploitation. Their employment in work harmful to their morals or health or dangerous to life or likely to hamper their normal development should be punished by law'. If this type of approach is implied when the sexual exploitation of children is discussed, then the reference is clearly to the employment of children in prostitution and pornography and excludes other types of sexual contact between adults and children, however unpleasant these might be.

The Supplementary Convention on the Abolition of Slavery, the Slave Trade, and Institutions and Practices Similar to Slavery, which was adopted by the Economic and Social Council in 1956, also makes a reference to exploitation. It condemns 'Any institution or practice whereby a child or young person under the age of 18 years, is delivered by either or both of his natural parents or by his Guardian to another person whether for reward or not, with a view to exploitation of the child or young person or of his labour.' There is little difference between this and Article 9 of the Declaration of the Rights of the Child. Although slavery is in fact a labour practice, this Convention widens the definition of exploitation to the social sphere, as has become usual in international labour legislation over the past 12 years with the recognition of an 'informal sector' labour market. Before this, it had only been possible to discuss exploitation in terms of exploiter/employer and exploited/employee. Recognition of the 'informal sector' involves acknowledging that, in situations of high unemployment and low social welfare, large numbers of people are driven to modes of income generating which are not wage-earning in the corporate sphere. Many of the trades, like street selling, workshop production and the petty service sector, are self-employed. What they have in common is low capitalization, low but rapid turnover, insecurity of income and lack of social benefits – many of the hallmarks of exploited low-paid workers. Moreover it can be shown that the 'informal' sector is functional for the corporate sector. It provides for the reproduction of a large section of the employed and underemployed waged labour force by keeping the cost of goods and services low and thus lowering overall wage levels. It also provides for the upkeep of large numbers of unemployed persons, who form a 'reserve army' of labour without the necessity of raising social welfare provision through taxation.

This type of overall exploitation of individuals who may be

formally unemployed, and only self-employed in the informal sphere, is referred to as social exploitation. This is also what is referred to in the Declaration of the Rights of the Child Article 9, which begins 'The child shall be protected against all forms of neglect, cruelty and exploitation'. Although this Article goes on to discuss child workers, the association between neglect, cruelty and exploitation is important. Like the idea of social exploitation, it allows one to think beyond the simple models of exploiter/employer and victimized child prostitute. This is clear in the Report made by Jean Fernand-Laurent as Special Reporter to the Economic and Social Council in 1983. Unlike Abdelwahab Boudhiba, who stressed economic exploitation of child prostitutes in the context of child labour using the traditional model, Fernand-Laurent discussed child prostitution within the wider context of prostitution of and traffic in all categories of person. As he sees it: 'The important point is not the scale of the phenomenon in terms of numbers but its degree of seriousness as a violation of the fundamental rights of the human person' (Fernand-Laurent 1983, p. 14). The exploitation he is concerned with has more to do with oppression than with labour practices: 'At the heart of the struggle for respect and promotion of human rights, a more specific struggle is to be waged for the liberation of women and children because they, together with the poor, are least equipped to defend themselves' (p. 36).

The category of 'the poor' should be linked also with racially oppressed groups, as will be seen later. At the moment, however, let us concentrate on what the international community regards as the proper means of defence for women and children. The form taken by protection, for children at least, is envisaged by the Declaration of the Rights of the Child as family life, as described in Article 6: 'the full and harmonious development of his [sic] personality needs love and understanding. He shall, wherever possible, grow up in the care and under the responsibility of his parents, and, in any case, in an atmosphere of affection and of moral and maternal security.' This, of course, is an ideal situation. As pointed out in the preceding Chapter, there is no universal family form. But moral abolutists, like Mrs Gillick, tend to act on the assumption that there is. Underlying the activities of many moral pressure groups is the same idea, which informs so much legislation, that the family must be protected as the best way of protecting children.

In an ideal world one could not help but agree. But the problem is that there is a great deal of evidence about the prevalence of intrafamilial sexual abuse. For instance, in 1981 a referral centre for sexually assaulted children in Australia reported that 40 per cent of cases of sexual abuse were incest, where the abuser was a member of the child's close or extended family. Other cases involved people known to the child through family contacts. Only 35 per cent involved children abused by strangers. 'Most children' the report concludes 'are abused by men they know' (Robertson 1983, p. 148). These results are replicated in other countries (e.g. Goodwin 1982; Finkelhor et al. 1983; Stern and Stern 1979; Ennew 1986), although some research indicates that the abusers are not always adults, even though they may be family members. The British Incest Survival Campaign has stated that 30 per cent of the reports made to them concern assaults on girls by brothers (Driver 1985). This figure must be qualified by the fact that it is gathered from self-reported accounts of women only. But paediatricians' accounts of their clinical practices relate many cases of sexual assault by adolescents on children (e.g. Ageton 1983).

Many examples of sexual exploitation thus take place while the child is within a family context and under the protection of its parents. On occasions the exploiter is the child's own parent, which further complicates the issue of sexual rights. It is not unusual for the sexually exploitative fathers, or less frequently mothers, to claim that parental rights over children include sexual access to the child's body and to add that parents are particularly sensitive sexual teachers (Russianoff 1981, p. 215). Sensitive or not, the resulting confusion can leave children with a conflict of loyalties. In the United Kingdom it raises dilemmas for doctors and Family Planning Clinics in the wake of the

'Gillick ruling'. Must a doctor refer to a parent in cases like the following?

> The girl in question was 14. She looked 12. She was living alone with her father – and she was pregnant by him . . . Her father had been having sexual intercourse with her for a year. Previous to that he had manipulated her sexually since the death of her mother six years previously. When she complained of the pain of intercourse, he burned her with matches – to show what *real* pain was about . . . She was petrified and the last thing she wanted was for her father to go to prison.
>
> The doctor said: 'It's fully understandable that she wants to protect her father. Whatever we think of him, in her eyes he is her provider, and also her lover'. (Lee 1985)

With cases such as this in mind children can only be protected if the non-ideal nature of much family life is recognized. The Draft Convention of the Rights of the Child shows a move in this direction by stating that children should be protected

> from all acts or omissions that are likely to be detrimental to the child's present or future welfare or development, including cruelty, injury, neglect, exploitation, discrimination and humiliating or degrading treatment, whether physical, psychological, emotional or sexual in nature, perpetrated by the child's parent(s), guardian or any other individual or social welfare institution responsible for the child's well being. (Article 8b in 1983 draft version)

The definition of child sexual exploitation is here broadened to include abuse and neglect within the family and not necessarily related to financial or other gain. This is a more realistic approach, but still deals only with protection. Should children also be protected from experiences like masturbation or mutual exploratory play? Do adolescents need protection from knowledge of sex and reproduction, or do they need protection from the consequences of experimenting with that knowledge? The issue of what is in the best interests of the child in sexual matters is unresolved. There is no provision for recognizing child sexuality, or for discussing whether this differs from adult sexuality or whether its expression should be permitted.

As with the question of child rights in general, in the area of the sexual rights of children there is a line of argument which runs counter to the theme of the protection of innocence. There are claims that child–child and adult–child sexual activities are both normal and desirable. This 'sexual counter-culture' is not new, but its present form in several countries of the developed world owes much to the libertarian ideas of what is often referred to as 'permissiveness' and the 'alternative society'. In some manifestations it is anti-family, regarding marriage, nuclear units and conjugal forms of child rearing as repressive and leading to personality disorders. At the very least, it has resulted in new attitudes to marriage, legitimacy, childbearing and both male and female roles. It has been associated with the idea that recreational sex is important and that women as well as men should enjoy it, that adults should not be ashamed of their bodies and of sexual acts, and that forms of sexual preference which do not involve heterosexual relations are acceptable. Some groups have attempted to find new communal forms of child rearing (Eiduson and Alexander 1978; Morin and Schultz 1978; 'Elisabeth and Ruth' 1977; Skolnick and Skolnick 1971). Many base their methods on ethnographically incorrect and romanticized theories of primitive societies. The 'golden age' of the noble savage and the 'golden age' of childhood are often ideologically joined.

As far as childhood sexuality is concerned, the counter-culture argument suggests that human beings have a life-long capacity for responding with pleasure to tactile stimulus. One psychologist in the United States asserts that children can be aroused by their own stimulus from the age of three and in response to the stimuli of others after the age of five (Martinson 1976, pp. 489–90). Erotic fantasies have been reported in children of both sexes from the age of four or five (Langfeldt 1979, p. 496). The child sexual liberation lobby has aimed to revise social attitudes and practices which repress child sexuality or which regard sexual relations between adults and children as immoral. Some groups like the Sexual Freedom League in the United States advocate only sexual activity between children and not across the generations. The Rene Guyon Society, which at one time claimed to have 3,000 correspondents in 45 States, advocated both kinds and asserted that transgenerational intercourse is not harmful provided that contraceptives are used. Based in California, this Group had some influence during the 1970s, when it campaigned to revise state legislation using the slogan 'Sex by age eight or else it's too late'.

Claims such as these may be partially based on ideas derived from developmental psychology. Some studies of the effects of sexual contact with adults seem to indicate that it does not provide either immediate negative reactions in children or long-term damage. Some writers point out that because most of the data on adult–child sexual relationships is drawn from criminal or clinical samples in which negative reactions are present, little, if anything, is known about the neutral or positive outcomes of such encounters (Constantine 1979, p. 505). Some evidence may indicate that negative reactions are the outcome of social taboos and guilt reactions in a society which punishes such behaviour. Ethnographic cases are used to show that such sanctions are not a human universal and that in some cultures the genital fondling of children by adults is part of routine nurture (Langfeldt 1979, p. 497). At least one psychologist reports that child–child sexual encounters are beneficial or even necessary: 'Most adults and youths with sexual dysfunctioning very often show deficient sociosexual engagement in childhood and adolescence' (p. 495). Negative reactions are reported to be the result of the use of physical violence, the child's ignorance of sexual matters and poor communication between members of the child's own family. One psychologist suggests that though non-abusive adult–child sexual relations are unlikely, they must be regarded as possible. The argument is that a rational legal framework would recognize that a child has a right to make a free choice of sexual partner, provided that the relationship excludes the use of force and is made with the child's informed consent. This places the burden of responsibility on the adult, who should ensure the child's informed and voluntary participation (Constantine 1979, p. 505).

The philosophical basis of the child sexual liberation argument is a criticism of repressive, patriarchal family models. New forms of child rearing and living groups are advocated, and sexual liberation is only part of a social revolution. In 1972 the Child Sensuality Circle was founded to dedicate its activities to the liberation of children in the widest sense, with particular attention paid to sexual freedom. Another organization, called Parents' Liberation, consisting of a group of 40 or more families divided into subgroups and practising familial sex, also saw child sexual liberation in the broader perspective of the achievement of other freedoms (Martinson 1976, p. 490).

Ideals of freedom in a Western democratic society have led to the development of many pressure groups which assert that they have the right to be liberated from previous attitudes and practices of social oppression. These groups tend to put forward arguments that their human rights to pursue particular options or have their value recognized by society have been consistently suppressed over time by the ideologies of a dominant majority, the main characteristics of which are white, middle-class, male, heterosexual and patriarchal. Majority does not necessarily have to be numerically proven – women are not a minority, numerically speaking, but in terms of human rights struggles are often regarded as a minority. The Black contribution to history is being consistently reclaimed as part of the liberation movement. Child liberation is a relative newcomer. The movement for the acceptance of the rights of gays in society has been particularly successful in gaining public acceptance for a way of life which was previously viciously repressed in many areas. The movement for paedophiliac rights has been less well received.

What all these movements have in common is an assertion that the characteristics of their group are not only normal and essentially human but also of value. Stephen Freeman, the former Chairman of the United Kingdom Paedophile Information Exchange stated in an interview that paedophilia 'has always been and shall always be as much a healthy part of our species as red hair or left-handedness' (*The Guardian* 5 December 1984). Two other leading members of The Paedophile Information Exchange were given jail sentences in 1984, after being convicted of sending indecent articles through the post and publishing an obscene article. The case concerned an article in the PIE Magazine *Contact!*, which contained an article about sexual intercourse with children and a letter which was also judged to be indecent. Both were professional men and had previous convictions for indecent assault on pre-pubertal children. The Judge in the case is reported as saying 'The law is designed to protect children. The most dangerous aspect of your organisation was that it sought to give an intellectual respectability to acts which society as a whole regards as loathsome' (*Evening Standard* 14 November 1984). As is the case with most reports of sentences passed on child sex offenders, the newspaper in which these words appear stresses the fact that the convicted offenders are likely to suffer at the hands of other prisoners. This story appeared on the front page under the headline 'Jail Fear of Child Sex Men', in letters one and a half inches high. One defence lawyer is reported as saying that the prisoners were in for a very hard time and that they had already been subjected to attack while they awaited sentence. A Conservative MP is also quoted as stating 'The prison authorities are going to have to be alert as far as these men are concerned. Even hardened criminals feel revulsion for people who interest themselves in the bodies of little children (*Evening Standard* 14 November 1984).

Approval or disapproval of the acts committed should not prevent a critical appraisal of this stereotype response. The argument relies upon the same reference to an absolute human nature as those used with more sophistication by some moral absolutists when they appropriate sociobiology. The MP is asserting that it is so basic to human nature to feel revulsion against transgenerative sexual acts, that these acts are *so* unnatural, that even people who are otherwise regarded as asocial or perhaps unnatural ('hardened criminals') will feel revulsion. There is no denying that child offenders receive rough treatment from other prisoners in many countries, particularly if the offences were committed against boys, but this is not necessarily the result of natural revulsion. It could be argued that other elements internal to the social structure of prison life come in to play. Because prisons tend to be single-sex institutions, many men and women who regard themselves as heterosexual become temporarily involved in homosexual relations, and feelings of shame may be associated with this. But child sex offenders have performed acts which are in general regarded as worse than homosexual relations, and venting anger on them may provide one means of expiating an otherwise unexpressed burden of guilt. Men who are separated from wives and children as a result of imprisonment suffer greatly not only from the guilt of their 'desertion' but also from the fear that their wives may have relationships with other men. How much greater is their fear and guilt if they consider the possibility that another man might violate their children? Moreover as child sex offenders sink to the bottom of the clearly defined prison hierarchy, so domination over them can give some kind of status to those whom society has condemned to powerlessness and from whom it may have removed almost all citizens' rights (personal communications and observations: sources suppressed).

The generally understood definition of a paedophile is an adult who likes and/or engages in sexual activities with a person under the age of 12 or, in other words, with a pre-pubertal child. A pederast, on the other hand, is involved with pubertal or post-pubertal adolescents between the ages of 12 and 16 (Rossman 1979, p. 216). In practice, the two are usually confused in everyday speech. In both cases what is important is youth, which may be experienced as sexual immaturity, as in the case of paedophilia, or a specific quality of freshness and becoming, in the case of pederasty. In the former case, the attraction to pre-pubertal children seems to have its roots in the adult's search for a lost paradise of his, or less frequently her, childhood. In this the adult seems to be overvaluing or mistaking the societal image of the 'golden age' of childhood in a specific, personalized way. Many psychoanalysts seem to argue that the tendency is related to an idealized version of the adult's own childhood, in which he remembers being the focus of uncritical, maternal admiration. A narcissistic vision of the self results – one with which society later does not concur. The paedophile is not attracted towards a real child or children, but to what these children represent as imagined replicas of himself as a child (Kraemer 1976, pp. 2–3). The inexperienced child, locked in a status in which all adults are powerful, offers no threat to the paedophile's immature personality, which is fixated on its own past and is unable to deal sexually with other adults who do not reaffirm the narcissistic image. Children do not compete with adults in these relationships and the paedophile can feel as omnipotent as he felt himself to be in his mother's gaze (Kraemer, 1976; Gordon 1976; Williams 1976). The relationships are often obsessive and may not lead to sexual acts or to sexual acts of a genital nature. Many paedophiles claim that the relationship is that of truly romantic love, and there would be few who disagreed with this if romantic love is defined as desire for an idealized person. Certainly there are many examples of adult–child relationships being represented in literature and the visual arts as the epitome of innocent, non-carnal love (Kraemer 1976, p. 7).

In spite of the idealization, clinical accounts show that paedophilic advances 'generally take the form of genital exhibition, verbal approaches through the use of exciting or shocking sexualised words, caressing the child's genitals, or persuading the child to manipulate the genitals of the adult' (Gordon 1976, p. 36). Since the advent of photography, it has also been possible for adults to preserve images of the child's innocent and immature body, even after the child itself has developed adult sexual characteristics. Paedophiles and pederasts often possess a large collection of photographic records of childhood and youth, which they are reluctant to destroy even when arrest is imminent (Tyler 1982). One of the unfortunate consequences of adult–child relations may arise from the transient nature of the child's attraction. It has been suggested that children who become involved with paedophiles may be vulnerable because they have not experienced affection and warmth in their family relationships. This loving relationship with an adult may provide their first sensations of self-esteem, yet the relationship is illusory because it is based upon their symbolic childish qualities and not upon their individual qualities. With the onset of puberty and the loss of their value as children they are likely to be rejected by the paedophile and this can reinforce the damage of earlier parental rejection and set up a pattern of self-devaluation for life (Kraemer 1976).

The love of pederasts for early pubescent and adolescent children may be based on similar immature personality traits and feelings of powerlessness to those experienced by paedophiles. But the illusion in this case is not the adult's own lost childhood, but the image of youth itself, and a specific aesthetic in which youth, energy, beauty and innocence are interrelated. It is not accidental that the common phrase used to describe both pederasts and paedophiles in English is a 'dirty *old* man'. Old age, as the composer's colleague Alfred says in Visconti's film *Death in Venice*, is the ultimate impurity. Thus it is not the adolescent's innocence which excites the pederast, but his or her purity. Childhood innocence is based in ignorance of sexuality as well as on physical immaturity. The adolescent, on the other hand, possesses not only more developed sexual characteristics, but also, in many cases, sexual knowledge. The difference between adolescent and adult is that between purity and impurity, between sexual knowledge and carnal knowledge. It is because of this that virginity becomes important in many ideologies.

Although children are *de facto* virgins, their virginity, and its violation, does not become an issue until they reach puberty. They are then in a crucial social position: particularly pure because they are on the edge of the irrevocable step into impurity. Virginity is often described as a concept which applies only to women, and certainly in societies where it is regarded as important it is used in the control of women, not only by men but also by the whole social group. As Kirsten Hastrup has pointed out, the biological fact of virginity enters a young woman's life as a social demand for a particular kind of virtue (Hastrup 1978). She suggests that women pass through three stages in life according to their sexual status:

Social category	Sexual status	Gender
Ambiguous	Virginity	Unspecified
Non-ambiguous	Sexually active	Woman
Ambiguous	Post-menopausal	Despecified

The special pleasure which is believed to result from breaching this ambiguity is described by Aldous Huxley in the thoughts of the priest Urbain Grandier, as he contemplates seducing the young daughter of his friend:

> Every young girl is potentially the most knowing of widows and, thanks to Original Sin, every potential impurity is already, even in the most innocent, more than half actualized. To help it to complete actualization, to watch the still virginal bud unfold into the rank and blowsy flower – this would be a pleasure not only of the senses, but also of the reflective intellect and will. It would be a moral and, so to say, a metaphysical sensuality. (Huxley 1971, p. 34)

In the twentieth century the symbolic power of virginity has been used to add the commercial value of at least one child. Film star Brooke Shields was bound by contract to remain a virgin until she reached the age of 20. The ambiguity of her status was further emphasized by the fact that she took part in sexually explicit scenes at the age of 12, while playing the part of a pre-pubescent prostitute in the film *Pretty Baby* (Goodman 1985).

According to Hastrup, men do not pass through similar stages – they are just 'men' all the time, but this is not entirely correct. They may be male all the time, but most societies have markers or stages through which males pass before they are socially accepted as men. In many societies, as Hastrup herself notes, a man is not a man until he has had sexual relations with a woman, and this is one of the vital factors in the development of double standards of morality for the sexes. A male virgin is thus similarly ambiguous, and this ambiguity is not only one of status but also of sexual identity. The beauty of sexual purity in a young male is part of a specific aesthetic which Voltaire, for instance, acknowledged at the same time as he denounced the 'vice of so called Socratic love': 'A young boy often resembles a beautiful girl for two or three years by the freshness of his complexion, the brilliance of his colour, and the tenderness of his eyes; if he is loved it is because nature is led astray . . . when his age has made this resemblance vanish, the mistake ceases' (Voltaire 1971, p. 32).

The virginity of boys is sometimes accorded a greater aesthetic purity than that of girls. Huxley imagines Grandier to be entranced not by a girl's purity but rather by her potential wantonness. Thomas Mann's novel, *Death in Venice*, is more concerned with a discussion of the aethetics of youth and age. The ageing composer von Aschenbach is obsessed with the form of the youthful Tazio. What is described is precisely the nostalgia for childhood and youth given in psychoanalytical accounts of paedophilia – less lust than hopeless yearning. Mann gives this a spurious intellectual respectability. This difference between the aesthetic purity of youth and the obscene impurity of old age is further emphasized in Visconti's indulgent film of the novel. The final sequence takes from the book the image of Tazio assuming a number of poses, silhouetted against the haze of sea and horizon. Mann understates the composer's death as he views this aesthetic perfection. In the cinematic version the purity of youth is contrasted with the obscenity of age: Von Aschenbach expires reaching out wordlessly to the boy and symbolically to youth, slumped in his deckchair in a crumpled suit, while black dye from his hair runs down the crude mask of makeup he wears in an effort to appear young.

As the examples here have shown, contrary to some popular stereotypes, not all paedophiles and pederasts are homosexual. Case studies in medical journals show that many could be described as bisexual (e.g. Kraemer 1976 *passim*). Moreover, even if they are homosexual, they are not necessarily male. Pornography for male heterosexuals has a teacher–schoolgirl genre in which adult females dressed in mock school uniforms willingly perform sexual antics with powerful schoolmasters who are empowdered to carry out various forms of corporal punishment. Similarly, pornography for the female homosexual audience often shows a return to school, particularly in the timeless all-female institution of boarding schools where, if power is exerted, it is in the hands of older women, and the socially acceptable ideas of wife and mother exist only in a funless future. It may be that youth for men and women has different connotations, the former conceptualizing it in terms of an aesthetic, unlike the latter who conceive of it as a time of lost freedoms. There are hints of this in the success of recent experimental holiday courses for women like the St. Bride's School in Donegal, where 'pupils' wear Edwardian uniforms and recreate a boarding school atmosphere and the head teacher is reported as stating that there is a 'need to recover a lost age of innocence' (Morris 1984).

Although it is incorrect to assume a correlation between homosexuality and adult/child sexual relationships, there are parallels to be drawn between gay rights and child rights. The use of the term 'Gay' denotes a change in attitude away from previous notions of sinful or diseased homosexuals. Similarly, the child rights movement points to a rejection of stereotypes of innocence and the first steps towards the idea that children are individuals with the right to exercise choice.

In this context some gay rights activists have suggested that their movement has important implications for children.

It is usually accepted that homosexual child play is more frequent than pre-pubertal heterosexual play (e.g. Kinsey et al. 1948). Childhood and adolescence are often referred to as homosexual phases, with same-sex preferences shown in affective relationships. Some interventionist child rearing programmes see it as important for parents to make consistent use of strong sex role stereotypes throughout childhood in order to prevent the development of homosexual tendencies (e.g. Wyden and Wyden 1968). Such approaches either imply or state openly that homosexuality is a negative identity option. Gay identity, on the other hand, is regarded as a positive adult option among others. Clinical psychologists Stephen Morin and Stephen Schultz state that there are no gay or homosexual oriented children and that gay or homosexual identity formation happens within the adolescent phase. The principles of gay rights applied to children do not mean that one must accept that some children are gay, but rather that one should consider the rights of the adults that children become; and some children do grow into gay adults (Morin and Schultz 1978, p. 140). It is important that the identity they choose to assume as an adult is perceived as a positive developmental outcome and not as deviant, negative or diseased. Thus Morin and Schultz suggest that socialization of children at home or at school includes showing the existence of a gay life-style option and its positive aspects 'in a context which neither discourages experimentation nor promotes any particular developmental outcome' (p. 145).

The Women's Rights Movement is occasionally linked with aspects of the Child Rights Movement. But few feminists acknowledge child rights to be a separate issue. Perhaps the existence of children is a reminder of aspects of traditional roles which many feminists are attempting to reject. Unfortunately it is common for women's rights activists, when they consider children at all, to assume that their rights are assured by adhering to feminist principles. Kathleen

Barry, for instance, states that 'separating child from adult female prostitution . . . continues to confuse the issues' (Barry et al. 1984, p. 24).

Although it is never possible to characterize the women's rights movement as one entity, the attitude of feminists to children's rights often takes the form of assuming the oppression of women and children to be identical in cause and manifestation. Thus a United States feminist, discussing child abuse and neglect, asserts that

> feminists have a better understanding than child welfare professionals of the causes and consequences of violence in families. Feminist analysis recognises abuse as rooted in unequal power relationships in the family and speaks to how women and children are victims of those relationships. This analysis has been translated into treatment programmes in women's shelters and other counselling programmes where women are encouraged to develop their own power and autonomy. (Washburn 1983, p. 290)

There are two problems in this refusal to disaggregate women and children as groups. The first is that it continues the association between women and children as minors in need of protection, which is a necessary correlate of male power. The second is that it does not acknowledge the importance of power relations based on age. Quite apart from the arrogance of the assertion that women as a group 'know best', and the assumption that child care experts are not female, writers with this sort of approach fail to understand that the 'analysis' that violence is rooted in unequal power relations is a fairly obvious observation, which predated any feminist theory. Moreover, if women do 'develop their own power and autonomy' it does not necessarily follow that children will automatically do the same. Indeed, the reverse is more likely to be the case. It has already been demonstrated that children are often treated as chattels of their parents in law. Removing the domination of fathers does not liberate children from adult domination, but can replace it with a new form of oppression. When feminists lay claim to rights over their own bodies, one often has the impression that this entails absolute rights over the products of their bodies – their children. The basis of the feminist argument against a private member's Bill to abolish illegitimate status, which was before the United Kingdom Parliament in 1979, was that it would give natural fathers the same rights of custody and access as natural mothers. It was clear that this feminist lobby was not advocating the best interests of the child in this, but rather the right of natural mothers to absolute custody and control over their children. The problem is that, although some feminists are correct to state that children and women are oppressed by the same forces, they fail to comprehend that the form oppression takes for children is different and that the repression of 'ageism' compounds the repression of sexism.

What are the alternatives offered to children if the cult of innocence is deconstructed? The protective approach aims to prohibit all forms of sexual activity between adults and children, and may or may not combine this with a prohibition on child–child sexual exploration, masturbation and sex education. There are three main arguments used to justify this attitude:

1 adult–child sex is intrinsically wrong;
2 adult–child sex entails a premature sexualization of what should be an innocent childhood;
3 adult–child sex damages children.

The first two arguments are merely assertions for which there is no supporting evidence. Indeed, as the first is a moral argument, it cannot be refuted or proven by empirical evidence. The second involves a confusion of moral and empirical issues. Empirical data regarding the last is by no means conclusive (Finkelhor 1979, p. 693). A great deal depends upon the form which sexual activities take and the age of the child involved. Physical harm need not necessarily result from genital stimulation without intercourse, or from intercourse with an adolescent, although post-pubertal girls are at risk of pregnancy. In cases where physical harm occurs, this can take the form of serious health problems: sphincter damage leading to loss of control, perforated vaginal wall, asphyxiation, venereal diseases including gonhorrical tonsilitis, anal or vaginal bleeding, urinary tract infections, pelvic inflammatory disease, enuresis and ecopresis, cervical cancer and perinatal complications (Barry et al. 1984, p. 90; World Health Organisation in Fernand-Laurent 1983, p. 32). Other children, who are not physically impaired, can exhibit a variety of psychosomatic symptoms, which vary with age and maturity, and behavioural problems (Vizard 1984 and figure 3).

Concern about the effects of sexual contact between adults and children usually refers to supposed effects on their subsequent psychological health and/or moral development. There are indications that some child prostitutes have suffered earlier sexual trauma, but this is not based on research using control groups (Gilbert n/d; Allen 1981; Janus and Heid Bracey 1980; Sereny 1984). A Canadian research report states that in a survey of 229 juvenile prostitutes in 8 cities, 'While some had been sexually abused as children, their experience in this regard was no different from that of other Canadian children' (Government of Canada 1984). In any case the moral development of children is poorly understood and there are no criteria for supposing that prostitutes are more morally degenerate than other social groups.

Because a child's sexuality is in the process of development concurrent with physiological, psychological and emotional development, it will be affected by all kinds of experience and much depends upon the context in which this occurs. If early sexual contact is experienced as part of a warm, affirmative relationship or is associated with physical pleasure, there is every reason to suppose that adult sexual life might be enriched. Sexual and other activities which are associated with pain and fear can be expected to have negative consequences. Because pain and fear are not simply of physical origin, feelings of guilt and confusion in childhood can also result in later psychological disturbance. It can be the case

Preschool

Physical Injury
Vaginal and anal lacerations and trauma. Genital bleeding, perineal inflammation and irritation. Other signs of physical abuse.

Medical Problems
Gonoccocal vaginal discharge, recurrent urinary tract infections.

Behaviour Problems
'Frozen Watchfulness' and overclinging, compulsive masturbation, oversexualized behaviour.

6–11 Years

Medical Problems
Recurrent abdominal pain, enuresis, encopresis.

School Problems
Conduct disorders, academic underachievement.

Psychological Problems
Excessive public masturbation, provocative oversexualized behaviour towards adults and children.

Adolescence

Behaviour Problems
Running away, promiscuity, pregnancy, social isolation.

Psychological Problems
Depression, suicide attempts and suicide, self mutilating behaviour, drug and alcohol abuse, homicidal rage attacks towards parents. Hysterical reactions.

Figure 3 Signs and Symptoms of Child Sexual Abuse:
A Developmental Spectrum
Note: Many of these signs and symptoms can be present at any stage in childhood, with the exception of pregnancy, depression and suicide attempts, which occur in the adolescent period.
Source: From Vizard E. 1984, The Sexual Abuse of Children — Part 2, in *Health Visitor* September 1984 Vol. 57.

that the actual physical acts of adult–child sexual relationships do little physiological harm and are associated with warmth and affection. Guilt and fear arise later when other adults or agencies discover the relationship and handle the 'offence' with insensitivity (Giovannoni and Becerra 1979, p. 242). Parents, doctors and police may react with shock and disgust to activities which the child had previously perceived as innocent. They may then prefer to cover up the occurrence and refuse to discuss it, so that feelings of guilt to which it has given rise may never be expiated.

The proponents of a sexual counter-culture claim that it is only the effects of repressive societal attitudes which cause damage in sexual relationships between adults and children. They claim that children have a right and a need to free expression of their sexuality in the same way as adults. But this provides children with no protection from exploitative practices and specifies little in the way of guidelines for adults who may wish to have non-abusive sexual relationships with children. It also only makes statements that children should *not* be taught the old repressive attitudes, and provides little in the way of positive precepts. It fails to develop an alternative morality beyond a libertarian 'anything goes'.

The key to solving the problem lies not in denouncing repressive morality, but in denying the premise of childhood innocence. Recognizing childhood sexuality does not necessarily lead to absolute sexual anarchy. On the contrary, it implies another form of adult responsibility in which both rights and duties are acknowledged. It also entails an 'implicit acceptance that children have a sexuality which can be exploited, and means that the approach is founded on children's needs at each stage of their development, as well as on their need for appropriate information and support at each stage' (*Children's Rights Monitor* 1982, p. 7). Innocent childhood needs to be broken down into different stages of development. Childhood sexuality should be regarded as different from adult sexuality not only because of physical differences, but also because of differences in knowledge and understanding of sexual activities and their consequences.

This is crucial for understanding the point at which sexual activity becomes exploitative in the wider sense. Within the tenets of the sexual counter-culture, a child's consent is regarded as important if relationships are to be non-abusive. In order to consent, a person has to understand the consequences fully and also be free to say no. Of course these two criteria do not apply in many adult–adult sexual relationships, particularly where power structures are involved, but they are particularly unlikely to pertain in adult–child sexual encounters. According to their stage of development, children possess differing information about the social rules surrounding intimacy and for judgeing the acceptability of sexual partners, as well as the social content of sexual activities and their physical and social consequences. Children can thus rarely give informed consent to sexual intimacy and there is a case to be made for protecting them from any situation in which they consent because of lack of information or false information. This does not entail protecting them from sexual knowledge but rather providing as much knowledge as possible in a form which is appropriate to their intellectual and psychological development. This will not brutalize them, but rather help to protect them from being brutalized: 'They have the right to expect not only that their sexuality be acknowledged, but also that they be provided with the means (emotional, material and informational) for coping with their sexuality and avoiding some of the devastating pitfalls that the lack of such means can have as consequence' (*Children's Rights Monitor* 1982, p. 7).

The second consequence of considering consent important is that because of their social status children do not have the same political or economic power as adults. Nor do they usually have equal physical strengths or capacities. Thus they are not as free as adults to consent or to refuse, and non-abusive or non-exploitative adult–child sexual relationships must be regarded as unlikely.

Children therefore do need to be protected from situations in which they might be manipulated or exploited. Education and open attitudes to sexuality may be one way of ensuring their protection, but we must remember that the age structure of society is not the only means of constraining children to consent to acts in which they do not wish to be involved. Just as children find it difficult to say no to adults, girls may find it more difficult than boys to say no to adult men, black children can be overawed into consent by white adults, and class differences probably provide the basis of the most insidious forms of manipulation at all ages.

4

Prostitution

Every harlot was a virgin once.
William Blake, *The Gates of Paradise*

Although all sexual abuse of children by adults can be regarded as exploitation and most of this abuse takes place with known or related persons, the main purpose of this book is to examine the facts and myths surrounding the sexual exploitation of children by third parties, for profit. The three areas in which this is believed to take place are prostitution, sex tourism and pornography. Each area presents problems for research. Children and adolescents who work as prostitutes are only a subgroup of a profession in which adults probably predominate. The lives of prostitutes and the economics of the activity have not been extensively researched and this is only partly because the work is clandestine. In some countries it is an organized, legal, taxable mode of gaining a living. It is not well researched because it is not usually regarded as a respectable or pleasant profession and this undesirability can and does reflect on researchers. Male investigators may be regarded as using a veil of respectability to hide a desire to be a customer; females can be regarded as tantamount to prostitutes themselves and thus be subjected to unwelcome responses from male colleagues, among others. Much of the limited information which has been obtained suffers from being based on hypotheses of social pathology which reflect societal disapproval. There is also a sense in which societies do not wish to know about prostitutes because the collective mind is already made up. Stereotyped images of 'fallen women', 'tarts with hearts of gold', 'nymphomaniacs', 'bad girls' and 'gold diggers' abound in literature, film and folklore, and research often reproduces these stereotypes. The form in which prostitution is thought about and institutionalized reveals not just attitudes to the sale of sexuality, but also the conceptualization of women, their roles and their sexuality. These images pivot on ideas of female sexuality, with which notions of homosexual male prostitution and child prostitution are compared or related: if female heterosexual prostitution is 'normal', male and child prostitution is 'abnormal'. Where laws exist to regulate female prostitution, they seldom include male and child prostitution, which are often dealt with under separate legislations. In England and Wales, for example, separate legislation deals with sexual acts between males and between adults and children – homosexual prostitution and child prostitution are not seen as subcategories of prostitution. Legislation about prostitution always assumes that it is female sexuality which must be regulated.

Prostitution is the institution of controlling or using an individual's sexuality for profit or gain. It does not include other institutions in which sexual rights are conferred as part of a monetary transaction, such as brideprice. The distinction is that marriage systems include the transferrence of a bundle of rights and duties, such as financial support, domestic duties and child rearing, which persist over time. Concubinage and keeping mistresses also include extended rights and duties on both sides, even though sex provides the principal rationale for these institutions. Prostitution, on the other hand, typically involves a contract worked out on market principles, for finite agreed sexual acts, whether the bargain is sealed in cash or in kind. It involves a buyer and a seller and thus reduces the complex individual mix of identity and sexuality to a commodity. The English name of this modern institution, like the name in most European languages, remains true to the Latin root *prostituere*, which meant to offer for public sale.

The common assumption, with which stereotypes usually concur, is that a woman's body is hired or purchased by a man for his gratification. There are few societal images of male prostitutes. Stereotypes of child prostitutes usually conform to an idea of precocity and seduction, in which unbridled child sexuality acts to corrupt an adult. Or it can assume the image of chattel slavery, in which a traffic in children steals them away from parents and keeps them in chains to cater for uncontrolled adult sexuality. Both images are mythological, despite isolated occurrences of each type. The first operates on the denial of child sexuality and consequent treatment of its manifestation as an aberration. The second uses powerful opposing images of family and strangers to reinforce not only the idea that the family is the correct locus for sexual activity, but also the need to strengthen the institution of the family as the basic unit of society. Both images depend upon an interpretation of sexuality as an uncontrollable force beyond the power of individuals.

A further assumption in the social stereotype of prostitution is that it involves acts of heterosexual coitus. Prostitution however can encompass a variety of situations in which sex is bought and sold in transactions with human bodies, but which do not necessarily involve either full sexual intercourse or heterosexual intercourse. Sexual gratification can be achieved in a variety of non-genital, non-tactile and non-heterosexual ways.

The institution is usually defended by two main arguments. The first is that prostitution is a 'natural' practice which has been in existence throughout human history. This could be called the 'oldest profession theory'. The second might be dubbed the 'male incontinence theory' and is often put forward by prostitutes themselves. The assumption of this point of view is that prostitution supports and reinforces the family as the basic unit of society, by functioning as a sexual safety valve for overwhelming male needs.

The first theory is simply not supported by ethnographic evidence. There are many historical examples of prostitution, and plenty of instances in non-Western societies, but there also seems to be ample evidence that prostitution is extremely uncommon in tribal and peasant societies. In any case, the use of the term 'natural' in conjunction with historical evidence is vacuous, particularly if it is used to justify the continuation of a practice. Torture and capital punishment have equally long histories, but the modern international community does not regard this as a valid reason to suggest that they are 'natural', much less that they should continue.

The 'male incontinence theory' entails the proposition that prostitution is a necessary social mechanism which ensures the persistence of the institution of marriage. It is based on the proposition that men have more powerful sexual desires and needs than women, and that these cannot be satisfied by the sexual activities permitted within marital relationships. Men have to seek release from these desires outside marriage and the most socially appropriate form of release is provided by contractual, marketed sex. Other kinds of extra-marital sexual relationships threaten the stability of marriage. After purchased sex, men can return refreshed to the cares of domestic life (e.g. McCleod 1982; English Collective of Prostitutes et al. 1981). It is also suggested that prostitutes are functional to society in relieving the sexual tensions of young unmarried men, who might otherwise enter unsuitable liaisons or marry too early. Thus the institution of prostitution is often referred to as a social sewage system: an unpleasant mechanism, which is nevertheless necessary in order to keep society clean. This idea has a long history: many twentieth-century writers claim that St Thomas Aquinas referred to prostitution as the social cloaca, a term which at that time was associated as much with the medical practice of purging as with drainage (e.g. *Perspectiva*, Lima 14 March 1982).

The 'male incontinence theory' has several consequences for the sexual status of both men and women. It is built on the assumption that there is a natural difference in male and female sexual desires and needs. Male desire is overwhelming, so much so that it threatens the proper conduct of social life. It cannot be controlled by the individual, but must be accommodated through a special social mechanism. The differential between natural male and natural female desires is so great that normal married women cannot satisfy their husbands' needs. Only prostitutes, who are abnormally sexed women,

can do this, and some prostitutes give this as a justification
for their work:

> Though it's her wifely duty to give them sex when they
> want – you'd be surprised how many dont. What's a
> man to do? He either gets involved with a girl which
> breaks the family up. Isn't it better he picks a prostitute
> up, pays for it and then forgets about it and dont get
> involved with a girl? Prostitutes save a lot of marriages.
> ('Michelle' quoted in Davidson 1982, p. 82)

The ubiquity of these theories gives the lie to the idea that the
separation of recreational from procreational sex is a recent
product of permissive society and modern methods of contraception. The separation has always been present in Western
society. It is produced by the division of women into 'good'
wives, who do not enjoy sex and have legitimate babies, from
'bad' whores, who enjoy sex and whose offspring cannot be
recognized as legitimate members of society. Some research
claims to support the idea that prostitutes are oversexed or
psychologically weak and therefore not suitable to be
incorporated into the respectable female society of wives and
mothers – the old English saying, 'the sort of girls you would
introduce to your father but not your mother'. For instance,
a psychiatrist and a psychologist from Latin America contri-
buted the results of their study of 50 prostitutes to a UNICEF
conference in 1967. They concluded that prostitution is an
expression of inner conflicts in immature and poorly adapted
personality types and that it is a psychological illness in need
of scientific study (Hernandez Aguyilar and del Pozo 1967,
p. 392). The irony in these theories is that it is the existence of
the sick prostitute which ensures the health of society.

Such theories degrade both men and women. Men are
regarded as persons unable to control their sexuality; women
either have their sexuality controlled within the institution of
marriage, or used and abused outside it. This type of theory
remains current in many 'Latin' societies (Arnold 1978;
Pescatello 1980), but is becoming increasingly unpopular in
cultures where feminist theory has penetrated popular ideas

of gender roles (Lindsey 1976). Yet even if it were proven, it fails to explain the existence of child prostitutes. On the contrary, it might be argued that a respectable husband and father would be unlikely to seek sexual catharsis with a child young enough to be his own son or daughter, without posing a major threat to the fabric of society. But if one accepted the logic of the 'male incontinence' argument, then one could also suggest that men might seek sex with child prostitutes in order to release themselves from incestuous desires for their own children. Thus child prostitution would appear to be necessary in order to preserve the family group and assure the sexual purity of legitimate sons and daughters.

One academic study of paedophiles suggests something similar to this, using ideas current in social anthropology. The proposition is that women are socially valuable objects exchanged between men at marriage, either by their fathers or their brothers (Pinard-Legry and Lapouge 1980, pp. 110–17; Lévi-Strauss 1969; Irigary 1977). As sexual objects, women are always either daughters or sisters and thus societal minors, hence marriage involves the exchange of social children and the control of their sexuality. The authors suggest that this is the origin of the horror expressed by families at instances of sexual abuse of children by strangers. Incest is less threatening than paedophilia, because it does not undermine the family's control of its children's sexuality, but paedophiles are direct threats to patriarchal authority. Because female sexuality is always, in a sense, the sexuality of a daughter, child prostitutes (whether male or female) do not constitute an abnormal market which has arisen out of satiation with normal sexual activity between men and women. On the contrary, child prostitution is a special case of the normal relationships of domination between men and women. It represents a particularly clear example of the values of family-based sexual activity – one which symbolises the 'totality of the economic and symbolic system' (Pinard-Legry and Lapouge 1980, p. 116). Even those who would not follow that line of reasoning to this conclusion may accept that shock campaigns on child sexual abuse are one way of emphasizing the need for families to control the sexuality of their sons and daughters.

The various attitudes of modern governments towards prostitution reveal the wide differences in cultural attitudes towards the institution. The main international instrument relating to prostitution is the Convention for the Suppression of the Traffic in Persons and of the Prostitution of Others, which was approved by the General Assembly of the United Nations by Resolution 317 (iv) on 2 December 1949 and entered into force on 25 July 1951. By April 1982, this had been ratified by 53 member states. The general attitude towards the practice is dealt with in the following Articles of this Convention.

Article 1. The parties present to the present Convention agree to punish any person who, to gratify the passions of another:

1. Procures, entices or leads away for the purpose of prostitution another person, even with the consent of that person;
2. Exploits the prostitution of another person, even with the consent of that person.

Article 2. Further agree to punish any person who keeps, manages or knowingly finances or takes part in the financing of a brothel.

Article 17. The Parties undertake . . . to check the traffic in persons of either sex for the purpose of prostitution.

Article 20. The Parties shall take the necessary measures for the supervision of employment agencies in order to prevent persons seeking employment . . . from being exposed to the dangers of prostitution.

The implication of the Convention is that to be a prostitute is not a crime and therefore not punishable by law. In fact, discrimination against prostitutes is specifically proscribed elsewhere in the Convention. It is procurement and profiting by prostituting others which are punishable acts. Being a customer for the services of a prostitute is not either a crime, or remarked on as a possible cause for discrimination. A further interesting point is that these articles refer to 'persons', who could be of either sex or any age. However, the preamble to the Convention refers to *women and children*, inferring that prostitutes are always either females, of any age, or male minors. The legislation is thus principally a protective measure for women and children.

Some governmental legislation reflects the spirit of this international legislation. But means of dealing with prostitution vary. Some governments favour containment of what they see as being an inevitable social ill; others make only certain forms, such as child prostitution or street soliciting, illegal. Some prohibit all forms but fail to eradicate the practice; others aim to abolish the practice by changing social attitudes towards women and sexuality (Fernand-Laurent 1983, pp. 16–18). Even among governments which take the same general approach, there may be variations in legislation about types of prostitution, the age(s) at which prostitutes may obtain a licence or be prosecuted, the penalty (if any) accorded to homosexual prostitution, the licencing or prohibition of brothels, and the penalties for procuring (ECOSOC 1984). There are countries in which it is denied that prostitution is a problem at all. When Bo Carlsson was researching child prostitution for the Anti-Slavery Society and Rädda Barnen, he received a reply from the Philippine government stating categorically that since prostitution is prohibited in that country 'it does not exist' (Carlsson 1984). Yet, as I shall show in Chapter 5, there have been reports of adult and child prostitution in the Philippines from many responsible sources. In a similar vein, the government of Qatar replied to a questionnaire sent by the United Nations Commission of Human Rights Sub-Commission on the Prevention of Discrimination and Protection of Minorities: 'We have the honour to report that such a problem . . . does not exist in our State. Our religion and our traditional heritage forbids such vices to take place anywhere in our State' (ECOSOC 1984, p. 15).

In contrast, some States not only recognize the problem but also regulate it. In West Germany, for instance, 'eros centres' are municipally organized, prompting the comment from one researcher that 'not only have finance companies found a new market here, but also the state has profited from these brothels [eros centres] through trade taxes' (Ohse 1984, p. 42). The rationale for licencing prostitutes is public health. It is stated that this inhibits or prevents the spread of sexually transmitted diseases, for a condition of registration is that licencees submit to regular medical examinations. One of the most disturbing of Toulouse Lautrec's many informal portraits of Parisian women at the turn of the century shows a line of bored prostitutes waiting to be examined by the state appointed medical authorities. The implication of such legislation is that, whether or not the prostitute is punished for her activities, it is she who must be regulated for she is the locus of social ill, literally translated as sexually transmitted disease. Clients do not need licences, nor are they regarded as the source of disease; and in the eyes of the law, the prostitute is always female. There are few states which license male prostitutes. Indeed male prostitution usually only enters the legislative spectrum under indecency laws, rather than laws against or about prostitution, just as legislation about the exploitation of minors in prostitution tends to appear under laws regarding the sexual abuse of children. Thus there are no states which license child prostitutes. Prostitutes with false papers may work in licensed brothels and this may account for some young women who work there under the age of majority or the legal age for licensing. In Peru, for instance, the age of majority is 18, but no one is allowed to work in or enter a licensed brothel under the age of 21. Girls who enter prostitution before this age work in clandestine brothels or in the streets. The prohibition is not applied to male clients of brothels. It is a tradition in many middle-class Peruvian homes to introduce boys to brothels once they have reached the age of 15, sometimes with disastrous effects on their subsequent sexual lives.

Thus the law concentrates on the prostitute rather than the

client, the vendor rather than the buyer, the female rather than the male. It is always the female prostitute who needs to have a licence in those states which regulate or contain prostitution. She is known to the authorities, while her clients remain anonymous; she has to submit to health checks, while her clients are free to spread disease. Although prostitutes are often the victims of violent behaviour by clients, they seldom complain of this. They are unlikely to receive sympathetic treatment from either police or courts of justice. Indeed many notorious cases of multiple killings, such as the so-called Yorkshire Ripper case, only receive maximum police attention once it is clear that victims can be 'nice girls' as well as prostitutes. Thus there is little likelihood that police would check up on a prostitute's complaints about a violent customer, and prohibit him from entering or using even a state registered, tax-paying brothel.

This discrimination against prostitutes is contrary to the spirit of the 1949 Convention, which prohibits such discrimination. It also occurs in those countries which either prohibit or restrict prostitution, rather than attempting to contain or regulate it. In the United Kingdom, for instance, both the 1956 Sexual Offences Act and the 1959 Street Offences Act were designed to counter the 'nuisance' of prostitution by increasing the legal penalties applied to convicted prostitutes. They attempted to sanitize the streets by preventing prostitutes from soliciting custom. It is only recently that legislation was put before the United Kingdom parliament to try to limit the activities of potential customers. The 1985 Sexual Offences Act, which attempts to counter the nuisance of men patrolling the streets in their cars, annoying women by importuning their services as prostitutes, was introduced only as a Private Member's Bill and had a very uneven passage through Parliament (Ansell 1984).

Thus, although prostitution is almost universally regarded as a social ill, only one side of the transaction involved is subjected to legislation. The client who buys sexual services receives no sanction for his half of the bargain, and his identity may even be concealed in court cases. The client is never seen as the source of disease. Whereas there have been many studies of the psychological and social problems which result in women offering their sexuality for sale, almost no studies exist of the social backgrounds and psychological makeup of customers. They may even be regarded as normal, though those with whom they trade are defined as sick, bad or criminal. Prostitution is an institution split by this fundamental ambiguity, which reflects or reveals the equally fundamental split in all societies between male and female, and its frequent expression in male control of female sexuality. The abnormal institution of prostitution is actually founded on power relations which are usually presented as normal or natural.

The few existing studies of clients seem to indicate not only that they are respectable societal members, but also that they tend to be relatively prosperous. This may imply that economic power relations are added to the control of female sexuality by males; but it could also be the result of a bias in research which may concentrate on the more easily penetrated networks of high-price prostitution, rather than more corrupt or underground forms. Fernand-Laurent hypothesizes that both the desire and the behaviour of the client arise from societal ideas and pressures. He indicates on the one hand notions of male virility and sexual potency which *require* men to seek sexual pleasure in order to be men and, on the other, ideas that it is a female duty to give pleasure. To this can be added the distinction between good wives and bad prostitutes and mistresses discussed earlier . He suggests that men may seek sexual services because they have received insufficient preparation for marriage and are subject to media pressures to seek particular forms of sexual enjoyment. He also stresses the importance of military service in the development of a client population.

Some of these factors are indicated in answers reported to a researcher by high-class call girls in India. According to these girls, 80 per cent of their customers were married men aged 40–65. Many of the reasons the girls gave as to why these customers should be purchasing sexual services were related to their respectable marital status and possibly the length of their marriages. They sought more unusual sexual experiences than could be obtained within their marriages, had insufficient sexual outlet through their wives, were frustrated, needed an 'inferior' or 'impure' sexual partner, and regarded the experience in the light of power and status (Kapur 1978, pp. 214, 221).

The clients of prostitutes in the Far Eastern market for tourists or other foreign customers show the same type of characteristics, according to the little research which exists. A PhD thesis from the Asian Social Institute states that the majority of clients of prostitutes in the Subic Bay area of the Philippines are military personnel. This is not surprising, given that this is the location of one of the largest United States bases in the area and has a long association with Rest and Recreation facilities for United States forces. But further examination of the evidence reveals that these clients have certain characteristics similar to those suggested by Fernand-Laurent. They are high-school educated and their primary reason for joining the armed forces is security, both for themselves and their future families. These men are family-oriented, rather than decadent and anti-family as might be suggested by moral crusaders. The predisposing factors for the use of prostitutes, according to this researcher, are the conditions of military life and a materialistic, hedonistic cultural orientation (Moselina 1978, p. 18). It may be that what we are seeing here is the manifestation of an essential contradiction between two fundamental ideals of United States culture. On the one hand the image of the close-knit, nuclear family group represents security based on the idea of people working together for group goals. On the other hand it is basic to individualistic, competitive notions of how societies and people operate that human rights involve the right to achieve pleasure, which is associated with happiness. If this were all the case, then it might be taken as proof of the thesis of moral campaigners that progressive, liberal ideas are breaking down traditional family values. But the indications from this research are that it is the same men who hold traditional family values who are customers for prostitutes.

Might one not argue an opposing hypothesis: that the institutions of the family and prostitution are interrelated in some way? Certainly historical evidence shows that both institutions are 'traditional'.

Research in the bars of Manila, the capital of the Philippines, may partially contradict this. A tentative survey of 50 males who were customers of prostitutes, carried out for Sister Mary Soledad Perpignan – one of the most responsible writers in this field – showed an average age of 39 among men of several different nationalities. Because they were foreigners abroad it is likely that these men would be middle-class, high-income and well-educated. This is indeed the case. Sister Mary Soledad reports that over half were college educated, half being graduates, but only a third had ever been married and most of these men were divorced at the time of interview (Perpignan 1983, pp. 16–18). Very few of the men interviewed in this research manifested a preference for very young girls or children, or male prostitutes. The vast majority were seeking sexual gratification with adult, female partners. Yet the evidence from research in the United States shows a certain similarity between these clients of prostitutes in general and adults who sexually exploit children. The same expert witness who claimed to the US Senate that child sexual exploitation was an epidemic, stated that the adults involved are likely to be 'White males, 50–60 years old, living in relatively upper income homes who are or have been married, generally tend to have from two to four children, and are making in excess of 35,000 dollars a year. They tend to be college educated and most are professional persons' (Allen 1981, p. 12). This profile is remarkably similar to that given by Judianne Denser-Gerber and S. F. Hutchinson in an article in the UNICEF publication *Ideas Forum* no. 16. They make no reference to specific research, but Dr Densen-Gerber has been involved in the rehabilitation of young prostitutes in the United States for many years and was one of the first to draw attention to the problem of child pornography in the 1970s. The article states that:

The men come from all classes and races though there is a marked Caucasian preponderance. Many are married – even those primarily interested in boys, and a surprising number are middle or upper class. Many are men of prominence and power. Some are jaded and bored, but almost all feel inadequate and unable to meaningfully relate to peer sexual partners. They see sex as something one person does to another, not as a mutually reciprocal relationship. Sexual activity equals a performance, and they relish an inexperienced child as a judge. (UNICEF *Ideas Forum* no. 16, p. 16).

Despite their obvious inadequacies, what these disparate pieces of evidence add up to is a reaffirmation of the assertion made in the first part of this book. Sexual exploitation is part of the wider spectrum of domination, in which rich exploit poor, males, females, whites other ethnic groups, and adults children. It also reveals a possible connection between family cohesion and prostitution, and draws attention to the fact that customers of prostitutes, even of child prostitutes, should be regarded as the subject of serious study. This is firstly because the market transaction of prostitution can never be understood while the customer is an unknown factor. But it is also because preventative work which deals only with the vendor will not eradicate the demand. We need to know what are the social factors which make men feel 'inadequate' and 'unable to meaningfully relate to peer sexual partners'. Moreover a sexual partner who thinks of sex as 'something one person does to another' is not only objectifying the person (adult or child) with whom he has sex, he is also objectifying himself. In sexual exploitation there are only victims.

If the sexual market operates according to laws of supply and demand, then it follows that there is a pricing mechanism which values some forms of sexuality above others. One needs to know if sex with young people, with children, with infants, with boys or with girls commands higher or lower prices than sex with adult women or men. It is also necessary to find out if the pricing mechanisms are related to particular cultural attitudes in the various countries in which prostitution operates.

An article by Daniel Campagna of Appalachian State University in the United States uses material from the so-called 'Meat Rack' report to derive an estimate of the gross revenue from child prostitution in the United States. Research for the report took three years and collected information from 596 police departments in 50 states, supplemented by a survey of 125 social service agencies and field surveillance studies of targetted cities. Campagna uses what he calls a 'very simple formula' to calculate the gross yearly revenue of the trade. It is based upon a 'conservative' estimate of $15 for a transaction, which is derived from the report, and employs a maximum–minimum range of variables, such as number of working days in a year. The table he derives provides a maximum and minimum value for the gross annual revenue of child prostitution activities:

Table 4.1 The Economics of Child Prostitution in the USA

Base number of prostitutes (V)	Working days (A)	Daily income (B)	Annual gross revenue (R)
V ×	A ×	B =	R ($000)
200,000	208/104*	$45/15†	1,872,000/312,000
150,000	208/104	$45/15	1,404,000/234,000
100,000	208/104	$45/15	936,000/156,000
50,000	208/104	$45/15	468,000/78,000

Notes:

*Estimated at maximum 4 or minimum 2 working days a week × 52 weeks.
†Estimated at maximum 3 or minimum 1 transaction(s) a day × $15.
Source: Campagna 1985, p. 000.

It is worth quoting Campagna's conclusions from this table at some length:

These figures are, to say the least, both enlightening and astonishing in their implications. The gross annual revenue varies from almost 2 billion to 78 million dollars, depending on the volume of the juvenile prostitutes selected for cross-indexing. Even at the lowest level (50,000 prostitutes corresponding to just 50% of the minimum estimated figure), the income is at least equal to, if not greater than, the gross national product of many developing nations. Keeping in mind that this table uses extremely conservative base figures for the A and B variables, the results clearly indicate that, in addition to being sexually used, child prostitutes are economically active on a systematic, unprecedented scale in the United States. (Campagna 1985, p. 15)

Despite Campagna's ingenuity, there are reasons to disagree with both his results and his conclusions. The use of terms like 'meat rack' in serious research on this subject has already been criticized. Campagna's methodological errors are more serious. The figure of 15 dollars per transaction is derived in the 'meat rack' report from evidence of police and social workers, not from either children or clients. As we shall see repeatedly later, children tend to prostitute themselves for very small sums, or petty goods. In any case, as it is possible to interview child prostitutes and clients, one wonders why the researchers did not do so. The assumed frequency given for transactions suffers from the same imprecision. A three-year investigation should not be satisfied with such poor data. In his conclusions Campagna is guilty of the typical scandalization approach. First he exaggerates: there are very few developing nations with a GNP less than two billion dollars. In any case, it is trivial and misleading to compare a consumer industry in a populous, rich nation with the GNP of a country with a population of less than a million. Then he draws false conclusions: nothing in the table he has presented leads to the conclusion that the trade he describes is systematic. Then he makes another false claim: because he does not present any comparative data he cannot possibly state that what he is describing is unprecedented. Finally he slips in another scandal for good measure: towards the end of his article he mentions sexual trafficking, coupling it with prostitution, although nothing in his discussion or data has related to traffic.

Modern images of 'Kiddie pros', even in relatively sober texts like that of Campagna, bear much relationship to the 'white slave trade' myths of the late-nineteenth and early-twentieth centuries. The difference is that the earlier version travelled from England to North America, while the present version crosses the Atlantic in the opposite direction. In 1885 British social reformer William Stead, in one of the many sexual scandals of the era (which included Jack the Ripper, the trial of Oscar Wilde, and the Cleveland Street scandal), wrote an article in the *Pall Mall Gazette* under the title 'The Maiden Tribute of Modern Babylon' which scandalized an England all too willing to be shocked (Rosen 1982). Stead had infiltrated the fashionable brothels of the time, and went so far as to prove his case by purchasing a girl of 13 for a pound for immoral purposes. One result was the change in age of sexual consent in England and Wales which has already been mentioned. American reformers took up the cause, and the claim that hundreds of women were being sold into slavery caused:

> a nationwide panic that reached its height during the years 1911–15. In the quiet of their homes, middle-class families devoured journalistic accounts of the ruin of young women in the hands of sinister procurers armed with poisoned needles and drugged drinks. Young girls, the headlines screamed, were being sold into virtual sexual slavery. (Rosen 1982, p. 112)

and

> Finally, posters appeared in conspicuous places in major urban areas with the warning: 'Danger! Mothers beware! Sixty thousand innocent girls wanted to take the place of sixty thousand white slaves who will die this year in the United States'. (p. 115)

Such comparative data seems to contradict Campagna's claim that present child prostitution is on an unprecedented scale, particularly if one bears in mind the lower overall population at the turn of the century when these notices appeared. Methods of estimation and induction seem to have changed little in the interim. In 1911 social reformers in Chicago published a report stating that US $15 million dollar's worth of business was involved in the traffic in women in that city (Rosen 1982, pp. 72–3 and Roe 1911, Appendix). The Chicago Vice Commission, which obtained the figures, derived them from multiplying the number of prostitutes on police lists by the average number of men the women saw, and again by the average price of each visit. Finally figures were included to account for rent of the brothels and sale of liquor on the premises (Roe 1911, p. 193; Vice Commission of Chicago 1911).

The effect of these stories in both eras has been twofold. First they tend to draw attention away from the small, but very real, traffic in women and children towards politically-oriented discussion of supposed increases in immorality. The whole issue tends to become an argument between exaggerating reformers and uniformed denials. Meanwhile the problem continues and there is little hope of its true extent or causes being discovered. More importantly the shock expressed within 'quiet middle-class homes' serves to accentuate their spurious security and to veil other, more deep-rooted socio-economic problems. In particular the sexual abuse of children within the family can be ignored.

In any discussion of the price of child sexuality, a distinction must be drawn between pre-pubertal child prostitutes and post-pubertal minors who are involved in prostitution. It has been observed that there is a strong preference for young people among clients for both male and female prostitutes. This may be related to the spread of the Western overvaluation of youthful characteristics, as well as to an association between youth, vigour and potency. This is not particularly Western or particularly modern, as the story of Abishag shows:

Now King David was old and stricken with years; and they covered him with clothes, but he gat him no heat.

Wherefore his servants said unto him, let there be sought for my lord the king a young virgin: and let her stand before the king, and let her cherish him, and let her lie in thy bosom, that my lord the king may get heat. (1 Kings 1, verses 1–2)

The efficacy of sex with a virgin as a cure for venereal disease is also a very widespread belief (Bhalerao 1984, pp. 202–3). But perhaps the most widespread, and Western-oriented, factor is the association of youth and beauty in popular culture. Even mature women who are described as beautiful are only thought of in this way because they appear to be younger than they are. Beauty is youth rather than truth in the 1980s. Thus youth raises the market price of sex in any context. The texts of male and female homosexual magazines reveal a tendency to refer to sexual partners as 'boys' and 'girls' rather than 'men' and 'women'. The same tendency is revealed in heterosexual magazines. This may be due to a cultural overvaluation of youth, a search for one's own lost youth in the sexual partner, or a reflection of the power imbalance implicit in much sexual activity. A further factor is the fear of losing, or desire to regain, the sexual excitement, energies and abilities of young people. Most prostitutes are young even if they are not teenagers or children. The average age of entry into the profession, according to the few studies available, is around 16–23 years old. Few prostitutes continue doing this work after the age of 30. This is partly because of the rigours of the work, which is often associated with alcohol and drug abuse as well as repeated pregnancies, or abortions, and sexually transmitted diseases. By the age of 30 many prostitutes have lost their attraction because of this and, because of the high value which customers place on youth, it is difficult for older prostitutes to earn sufficient income. Among prostitutes' organizations this early redundancy is a frequent complaint. In the Peruvian port of Callao, a group of prostitutes calling themselves Movimiento el Pozo (The Well Movement) went on strike in 1982 to protest against their replacement in the brothels by younger women.

Most available evidence about child prostitutes refers not to pre-pubertal children but to young people who have not reached political majority. There is a market for young children, but I would suggest that it is not as large as moral crusaders would wish us to believe. Nor is it necessarily the basis for a profitable industry. Pre-pubertal child prostitutes may be part of either low- or high-priced prostitution. Paedophilic customers are specifically interested in sex with children, partly to recapture their own idyllic and narcissistic image of childhood, partly because children are not seen as threatening sexual partners. Theoretically it could be argued that they might be willing to pay a high price for this contact, and they might have to if supply were low and demand high. This is a specialized market, which could raise the price a little, but supply is not all that low and the market is also limited because paedophilia is related to romantic ideas of love and childhood. Purchased, short-term sex is not the most gratifying form for paedophiles and they are more likely to seek a longer term relationship with a child they know.

The other market for pre-pubertal sexuality is particularly cheap and arises out of the availability of children for both sexual and economic exploitation in certain contexts. It has been estimated that some 7.7 million vagrant children live beyond adult care or control in urban areas of many countries (Anti-Slavery Society 1985). They are particularly vulnerable to adult exploitation, and available for cheap sex to customers who are not primarily paedophiles, but who simply seek sexual gratification of any kind for the lowest possible outlay. These customers are not usually rich degenerates but poor, unemployed, and possibly homeless men. The attraction of children may be simply that they are the only sexual partners available to men who appear to be social failures and that the child's social status and small size provide a means of exercising power which is otherwise not available to them. Street children may be exploited by adults or older youths who act as procurers and provide the children with food, drugs, shelter and a fiction of adult protection. On the other hand, children may sell their own sexuality directly to casual customers, often for as little as a packet of sweets or a handful of cigarettes.

The price mechanism of prostitution is not just related to the relative age of prostitute and client, but also to the type of act for which the price is paid. The little evidence that is available seems to indicate that prices are set in relation to a norm of heterosexual, simple acts of coitus between an adult male and a young woman. Higher prices may be paid according to the act, the partner or the circumstances. Thus masturbation is paid less than coitus, which is cheaper than anal intercourse, whether this is heterosexual or homosexual. Different prices are paid for the age, sex or number of partners involved, and real or apparent virginity can be included in this. The circumstances may vary from waste ground or street doorways to luxury hotels and apartments. Special features of acts may include such tastes as whipping and humiliation, and refinements in costume and speech. The act or acts for which the contract is established may involve a time-scale of moments, hours or days. Some prostitutes specialize in particular acts, or clienteles; many refuse to perform acts like anal intercourse or bondage; some specialize in masturbation and will refuse to take part in coitus.

It is this variation in the market which makes nonsense of guestimates like the 'meat rack' report. It is also clear that, even though child prostitution may take place on a wide scale, it is not a hugely profitable industry. The casual child prostitute, who sells him or herself for purchase of drugs or other consumer goods, together with vagrant children lowers the overall price of prostitution. The mechanism is the same as that by which child labour everywhere operates to keep adult wages down. Children do not have to support families, houses and rents. They are involved in day-to-day target earning, for the price of a meal, a visit to a cinema, drugs, records and clothes. Adult clients are not likely to seek a high-price organized industry in child prostitution when they can find children and young people willing to sell their sexuality cheaply and without the intervention of an adult entre-preneur. The most shocking facts about child prostitution are not derived from its supposed control by vice rings, but from its petty, sordid reality. Why are young people willing to sell their sexuality for so little gain? Why are some adults seeking such paltry sexual gratification?

Almost the only first-hand account in existence of the life of a child prostitute describes the career of a 13-year-old West German girl who prostituted herself at the Bahnhof Zoo and the Kurfurstendamm tube station in West Berlin in order to purchase heroin. The story of 'Christiane F' has been widely translated and also turned into a film. It is clear that her work was not organized by any pimps or brothels – in fact she describes the violence of adult prostitutes who tried to pre-vent her from working ('Christiane F.' 1980, p. 190). She was not abducted from her home, and continued to live with her mother during most of the time when she was working as a prostitute. Gitta Sereny's selection of case studies of child prostitutes in West Germany, the United States and England provides much the same sort of picture. Even though many of the children she describes were working under the control of pimps and some had been lured away from home, there is no evidence of the operation of vice rings or a vast industry. Some customers in both books seem to be attracted specifi-cally to children, but most seem to be looking for youth rather than childhood for the services they purchase (Sereny 1984).

The families of children in these case studies are neither particularly moral nor particularly immoral, but there are some indications that there is a correlation between certain forms of family life and child prostitution. This operates at the level of supply rather than demand and precisely in those societies, or classes, for which the nuclear family has become the ideal if not the norm. Studies of child prostitution in the United States (Davidson 1982) and Europe (*Femme et Monde* 1981, 1982, 1984; Sereny 1984) suggest that many children become involved in prostitution after they have run away from home. In many instances, children who have fled difficult home environments travel to conurbations or metropoli in which they will be anonymous, only to find themselves friendless and homeless. The organization SOS Enfants estimates that there are about 5,000 boys and 3,000 girls working as prostitutes in Paris, many of whom have entered the trade after leaving home. As discussed earlier (p. 4), Lloyd's study of boy prostitutes suggested that there were 300,000 boy prostitutes in the United States, most of whom are designated runaways (Lloyd 1979). The journalist Gitta Sereny suggests that an unknown number of the 13,000–15,000 juveniles who are reported as missing from home in the United Kingdom each year could be working as prostitutes (Sereny 1984).

Whilst many child prostitutes are runaway children, not all are living outside a family group. It is important to realize that a home environment which ensures that children are well-fed, adequately clothed and in good health does not necessarily prevent a child from becoming involved in prostitution. Some children prostitute themselves in order to supplement pocket money (Sereny 1984, part 2). Others leave materially wealthy homes because of disputes or emotional problems. Casual prostitution applies to cases of children whose livelihood is not primarily connected to prostitution, but for whom it provides some extra income or pocket money. They may be runaways, or continue to live at home. It is important to remember that there is some element of choice involved. Children living at home decide that their need for certain consumer items, like clothes, records or tickets for discotheques, is sufficient to make it worthwhile for them to sell their sexuality. They discover the cash nexus of market and prices, their roles being those of both seller and buyer. Christiane F., describing the effects of prolonged heroin abuse, wrote 'Now I only felt good when I dreamt, and in my dream became someone quite different. What I liked to dream best was that I was a cheerful teenager, as cheerful as in a Coca Cola advert' ('Christiane F.' 1980, p. 136). Throughout the book she appears disgruntled, constantly complaining about the material things her mother failed to provide, always looking for the next purchase or release from boredom. She was not pressurized to take heroin, and took the decision to prostitute herself in order to support her habit, but this must be considered a special sort of choice, determined as it is by social ideas about women, children and sexuality.

This type of casual prostitution is most likely to be prevalent in developed societies, and is a result of relative wealth rather than relative poverty (although it has been noted among upper-class girls in developing nations). Sereny provides the case of two English girls who sell themselves on Friday evenings and Saturday afternoons, in order to make enough money to pay for the weekend's entertainment of clothes purchases and disco dancing (Sereny 1984). Other reports suggest that this type of casual prostitution, perhaps conducted after school hours or when children are truanting, is also prevalent among boys. One local paper in Northamptonshire in the United Kingdom recently reported that boys from the age of 13 upwards, waited for customers outside public lavatories, amusement arcades, hotels and cafes, waiting for clients who came from a wide variety of social backgrounds (Redley 1984). In the very different culture of the Amazonian town of Iquitos it has also been reported that schoolgirls in their mid-teens work in clandestine brothels, with the idea of earning enough money to improve their social situation in a society increasingly dominated by consumer values (Alves-Milho 1977, pp. 29, 44). In Singapore, schoolgirls have been reported to be working as prostitutes at weekends in order to support their consumption of illicit drugs (Lebra and Paulson 1980, p. 48).

Ironically, it is because children are protected by laws preventing them from seeking full-time employment under a certain age that they are likely to be forced into prostitution if they run away from home. This is particularly true of developed societies, in which there is not a wide variety of informal sector trades to choose from. Runaways in the poorer countries can enter a range of different street trades, which ensure the survival of a large proportion of the population in situations where formal employment opportunities are rare, and social welfare almost non-existent. But developed societies, in which welfare systems are better developed and employment is more strictly regulated, offer few opportunities for income generation outside the formal sphere, other than in illegal practices. By living outside institutions or family care, runaways become deviant societal members and thus entry into the illegal labour force inevitably follows from the act of running away. Of all the trades available to children in these circumstances, prostitution is probably the easiest and most lucrative.

In a study based on 12 years of research into child prostitution and pornography in the United States, Janus and Heid Bracey (1980) identified three broad groups among children who leave their home environment:

1 *runaways* who persistently and determinedly leave home;
2 *walkaways* who come and go from their homes;
3 *throwaways* who are rejected, or whose absence is of little or no consequence to their parents.

The findings of this research also suggest that the majority of children involved in prostitution come from households with one or more of the following characteristics:

• the family is non-nuclear (73%)
• there is parental drug abuse (26%) or alcohol abuse (60%)
• there was sexual abuse in the home (64%).

As with the majority of studies of child prostitutes, however, there is no control sample in this research and evaluation is difficult. It is impossible to say for instance how many homes there are which have these characteristics but in which the children are not involved in prostitution. In Western societies, at least, it seems that children from any socio-economic background may become involved in prostitution. Moreover, it is not only children from broken or economically impoverished homes who run away. Children from comfortable backgrounds are as susceptible as any others to crises of adolescent rebellion and intergenerational misunderstanding. Gitta Sereny notes the way in which many of the parents of prostitutes she interviewed had agonized over their own culpability (Sereny 1984, *passim*). Yet evidence for all assertions of this kind is scant. Studies like that of Janus and Heid Bracey are usually small-scale and deal with specific populations with no control group. There is no reason to generalize from their results to child prostitution as a whole, and anecdotal evidence which has been gathered from extensive interviews is probably of more value than surveys conducted on small samples. Certainly there are no causal inferences to be drawn at this stage. One can simply note that there may be a relationship, for instance, between non-nuclear families and runaway behaviour in offspring. Likewise there is some indication of an association between drug and alcohol abuse and child prostitution. Many children who sell their sexuality either use drugs themselves or have friends and sexual partners who are drug or alcohol dependent. There is also evidence that parents (possibly living in nuclear families) will prostitute their children in order to support their own addiction to either drugs or alcohol (Baker 1980, p. 302; Gersen 1979, p. 36).

Most runaway girls who become prostitutes enter the trade through their relationship with a man, who will be their first pimp. One reason for this is that the pimp can provide false identity papers, through which minors can evade prosecution, and even work in legal brothels (Sereny 1984). The young runaway's relationship with her pimp is complex (McCleod 1982). The man initially provides protection and affection for the girl, who may have lacked parental affection: 'The pimp builds upon the family model, with himself as the exploiting father. Girls are given names within the group, as wives-in-law, or girls who are not in the same stable and who do not have a pimp, are called outlaws. This new family structure is, for many girls, all the family they have in the world' (Janus and Heid Bracey 1980, p. 5). These runaway girls may be running from their homes, but they may also be regarded as running to a fiction of family life. Later, a girl's emotional dependency may have become such that she remains with the pimp, even if his apparent affection is withdrawn, if other girls join his 'stable', or if he resorts to violence. The pimp plays a subtle role to win the loyalty of the girl he has chosen. The girl gradually becomes emotionally dependent on the man to the extent of agreeing to prostitute herself for his benefit. This pattern shows little variation, whether it takes place among runaway girls arriving from the countryside in London, Paris, New York or Mexico City. Once involved in prostitution, the girl can extricate herself only at the risk of losing the spurious stability she has found, even if she is under no threat of physical violence. Most leave only to go to another pimp, and many retain affectionate memories about their first protectors, which are belied by the facts of the actual treatment they have received (Sereny 1984 *passim*). A Minnesota police officer made the following analysis of the relationship during an interview with one researcher:

> 'the pimp–whore relationship is a very precise one, with rigorously defined and mutually accepted conventions. The primary one – a fundamental part of the game – is that she denies even to herself that he cheats her; and at the same time, she never cheats him. If she does, he punishes her, and in this morbid and pathological relationship she expects and even provokes the punishment . . . this dishonesty . . . is not just part of, it *is* the relationship. It is the emotional corruption which the young girls find almost impossible to erase or reverse, even if they manage to break away from the life.'
> (Sereny 1984, p. 70; see also Gray 1973)

Runaway boys also enter prostitution through a system of adult patronage. Lloyd tells of boys in America who are picked up and befriended on their runaway journey by adult men (Lloyd 1979, p. 29). The boys are offered a comfortable place to stay, good food and a good 'start'. Sex enters the relationship only gradually, as friendship and trust develop, and clients will not be introduced until a later stage. But there are distinct differences between girl and boy prostitutes in this matter. The girl's protector, father figure and pimp contrasts with the boy's patron (URSA 1981). The man–boy relationship does not always rely on the man explicitly buying sex or selling the boy to other men, but may be cast more in the mould of a love affair for both parties: 'The majority of girls' clients want nothing beyond a quick and anonymous release, but many homosexuals seek relationships even when on the prowl' (Sereny 1984, pp. 221–2). Boys who sell their sexuality are more likely to have no protector, and are thus often more involved in networks of violence (URSA 1981).

Although many children are casual prostitutes, organized prostitution of children and young people takes place in many countries and in various forms. 'Organized' implies types of prostitution in which children do not operate by themselves to form liaisons with clients, but work with pimps or through brothels. Some children may exercise an element of choice in becoming part of an organized prostitution business, but many young prostitutes are deprived not only of all autonomy in the choice of sexual partners, but also of all control over remuneration. There are numerous examples from various countries, few of which can be meaningfully compared. One of the best documented among developing nations is the case of Thailand and, in the present state of knowledge, it can be taken as a fairly typical example of what happens in a situation of poverty in which prostitution is illegal (as it is in Thailand).

It is estimated by Thai sources that there are over a million prostitutes in Thailand. The overwhelming majority of these are young women. Of those under 18, 35% are 17 years old, 55% are aged between 15 and 16, and about 10% are 13–14 years of age, although some are even younger (Lebra and Paulson 1980). Most are the daughters of smallholders or labourers in depressed and remote rural areas, lured to the cities by recruiters, who claim to be from an employment agency and offer advances on wages to the parents. Once in the city, the girls are subject to tight controls amounting to virtual imprisonment, physical abuse, long working hours and well below subsistence wages (Anti-Slavery Society 1984).

In January 1984, five young prostitutes died in a fire in a town in Phuket province. One girl had been bought from her parents for 6,000 baht (US$33) 'advance' on her wages for unspecified work. Shortly after this, she had sent her mother a letter saying that her future was ruined, that she had been beaten and forced to prostitute herself. Her only escape would have been to redeem herself with the 6,000 baht, but her mother had already used the money. Another 15-year-old girl injured in the fire had been sold for 8,000 baht (US$43) and told that she could redeem herself for 20,000 baht (US$109), but at 10 baht per customer (about 5 cents), even considering that each girl was expected to service 5 to 10 customers in a 12-hour working period, her freedom seemed unlikely. Although there are legal sanctions against this type of traffic and trade, the fines are ridiculously low: 3,000 baht (US$16) for a recruiter and 4,000 baht (US$22) for a brothel owner or operator. Very few prosecutions are made and bribery and protection are alleged to be commonplace (*Human Rights in Thailand* 1984 vol. 8 no. 1, pp. 22–6).

In the urban areas of South East Asia unemployment is high and formal sector employment unlikely for unqualified rural girls. But, because of the existence of a wide variety of informal sector opportunities, these girls do have a greater range of choices available than underage runaways in a more organized labour market. Nevertheless, the conditions of work and pay in sweatshops may make bar work and prostitution seem a more pleasant alternative. A study of Philippino bar girls states that a female factory worker earns on average 320 pesos a month compared to the average nightly income of a bar worker at 55 pesos, to which one can add 200 pesos for each sexual customer (Wihtol 1982). Thus wages can be relatively better despite the fines which bar girls have to pay for misdemeanors like arriving late.

The Anti-Slavery Society has recently reported two instances in Thailand where brothels were raided by police and children released from a captive life of forced prostitution. The first case concerned a brothel in the Tha Muang district of Kanchanburi in Central Thailand. Twenty-nine girls aged between 14 and 19 years old were released. The girls had also been shipped once a month to Malaysia in order to entertain customers there. In the second case, a brothel in Ban Pong district of Rachaburi province was found to be employing 13 girls (Banerjee 1980, p. 36). Whilst young hostages may be released from forced prostitution by the efforts of the police, it seems that corruption may ensure that those people responsible for running the brothels and imprisoning children may escape punishment.

Organized prostitution in Thailand includes very young girls and boys as part of its clandestine operations. Child prostitution is part of the overall structure, not an institution apart. This is also the case in other countries like Brazil and France (*Revue Abolitioniste* 1981), Peru (*Creatividad y Cambio* 1981), India (*Depthnews* 1982), the United States, West Germany and the United Kingdom (Sereny 1984). It is the procurers and pimps who play the most important role in supplying young girls to the customers by providing false identities for the girls (Heid Bracey 1979). Whether prostitution is prohibited or state-regulated, it is usually vitally necessary for girls to prove that they are over a certain age and thus legally available for sexual activities or sexual commerce, or simply old enough to live independently. For false identities to function, official bureaucracy and policing have to collaborate at some stage with pimps and procurers. Clandestine young prostitutes could not be used in any country in the world without some level of corruption within authority structures

Studies of prostitutes are rare, and the methodology tends to be poor. Samples are usually small, with questionnaires badly constructed and no control group. Comparison between studies is impossible. Yet, from this evidence, it does appear that it is common for girls to begin prostitution as minors. Evidence about pre-pubertal or pubertal youngsters is scanty and nearly always derived from a Western social context. The following studies give some indication or incomparability and poor research techniques.

In the United States some studies have been made of small groups of child prostitutes, usually by psychologists, and one can add to this data from studies of adult prostitutes. Silbert (n/d 1970s–80s) studied 200 street prostitutes in San Francisco and found that 70% of them were under 21 years of age. Of these, 60% were under 16, and some were only 10 or 11 years old. Some of the older girls had started work under 16. Many reported a family background with alcohol abuse (50%) and incest or sexual abuse (61%), which had usually taken place around the age of 10 years old with a father or father figure. Ernest Allen of the Jefferson County Task Force, giving evidence about his work in Louisville to the United States Senate, stated that girls and boys who are exploited as prostitutes can be expected to be of average intelligence, from a blue-collar background and aged 11–16 (Allen 1981). He concentrates on characteristics of the family and claims that in general it will show a high degree of racial prejudice. He does not give any breakdown for the racial composition of his group. Silbert, on the other hand, found that his sample was 69% white, 18% black and 11% hispanic. But, without knowing the racial composition of the overall population of San Francisco this information is useless. In addition to being racially prejudiced, the families Allen describes are 'problem' families. Eighty per cent are headed by a single parent, although his definition of this includes mothers who are 'either dating or remarried and working'. Given this imprecision, one views his categorization of 18% of the families as 'warm' and 53% as 'hostile', with some uncertainty. But, in view of the fact that 90% of his group are defined as runaways, it is not surprising to learn that 90% reported physical abuse from parents and 50% claimed to have been sexually abused. The average age at which they had first experienced intercourse was 12 years old. Janus and Heid Bracey, after twelve years of work with prostitutes in New York, found that 82% of their sample had had intercourse before the age of 13, the youngest being 9 years old. Their information is derived from adult women who were working full-time in pornography or as prostitutes. As seen above, the majority came from non-nuclear families (73%) and homes in which they had suffered sexual abuse. According to their accounts, 60% of their parents abused alcohol and 26% were drug abusers. From these three geographically distant examples, using different samples and methods it might be tempting to conclude that sexual abuse at home is associated with subsequent child prostitution, but without any kind of control group this would be unwise. Moreover, a Canadian Government survey of 229 juvenile prostitutes in 8 cities states that: 'These youths came from families in all walks of life. While some had been sexually abused as children, their experience in this regard was no different from that of other Canadian children' (Government of Canada 1984).

With such variations in the data from North America, it is not surprising that it is even more difficult to draw conclusions from studies which have taken place in the developing world. Researchers in each country tend to reflect the cultural concerns of their nation when they devise their methodology as well as when they interpret their findings. North American research seeks correlation with family dysfunction in the form of non-nuclear households, or irregular behaviour like drug and alcohol abuse, as well as sexual abuse of children. But a Peruvian sociologist working with 400 licensed prostitutes in Lima was concerned with whether or not they were part of the huge rural–urban migration, how many children they had, whether they could read, and their racial group. All these questions reflect Peruvian social concerns – a prejudice against rural migrants and people of Indian inheritance, and the idealization of motherhood which is characteristic of machismo culture. The findings were that only 38% of these prostitutes were rural-born, 22% had completed secondary education, 72% were of mixed blood and 37% had more than two children. Few of the researcher's hypotheses were confirmed but he compensated by concluding, without any evidence, that prostitutes have weak personalities, are egocentric and materialistic, and are the product of defective socialization due to a conflict between traditional and modern ideas of womanhood (Ismodes 1967). Just as North American family research is dominated by ideas of non-nuclear family forms as pathological, so its South American counterpart is influenced by the strictures of 'machismo'. Nothing in any research carried out so far on child prostitution gives any more than glimpses at the sort of factors which bring about the phenomenon; nor is one left with any real idea of the dimensions.

5

Sex Tourism and Traffic

And now, what will become of us without barbarians?
They were a kind of solution.
C. P. Cavafy, *Waiting for the Barbarians*

Around the middle of the eighteenth century, journeys of exploration made by European travellers began to be regarded as tours. They were still exotic, but sights first seen and described by pioneers were now available for review and redescription by people who sought specific types of experience, through travel to areas and among peoples which could be regarded as different from themselves. Two interlinked factors which enabled this process to take place were improved transport technology and the spread of effective administrative government. Shortly after the Act of Union which linked the English and Scottish polities in 1770, Samuel Johnson made his ponderous way to the Hebrides, to look at the inhabitants. He wrote that 'Till the Union made them acquainted with English manners, the culture of their lands was unskillful; their tables were coarse as the feasts of the Eskimeaux and their houses filthy as the cottages of the Hottentots' (Johnson 1775, p. 41). Unfortunately, his preconceived notions of the sights he was about to see were doomed to disappointment, like those of many more recent travellers. He was unable to encounter examples of either noble or ignoble savages among the lairds, tacksmen and tenants with whom he stayed. Somewhat sourly, he remarks that 'a longer journey than to the Highlands must be taken by him whose curiosity pants for savage virtues and barbarous grandeur, (p. 90). Literature and travellers' tales continued to draw visitors to Scotland in search of savage simplicity, just as myth and legend cast a spell over travellers in search of

the classical Mediterranean. Travellers' guides, which delin-
eate and prejudge sights for visitors, began to be published
early in the nineteenth century and Thomas Cook's tours and
excursions started in 1841 (Turner and Ash 1975, pp. 51–9).

The first tourists tended to be people of the leisured classes,
who regarded a Grand Tour as part of the education of ladies
and gentlemen. The changes made by Cook opened up possibilities for the slightly less wealthy, not only for reasons of
absolute cost, but also because of efficiency. With Cook's
organization, travellers who had less time to spare from commerce and industry could reach more distant places. But true
mass tourism did not appear until the advent of workers'
holidays and improvements in wages and conditions for the
Western working classes. Mass tourism led to the development of tourist resorts, which have the sole purpose of
diverting and entertaining visiting holidaymakers. Since the
Second World War, which had the effect of transporting vast
numbers of working class men of all nationalities to distant
lands and cultures, leisure travel to foreign places in search of
relaxation and new experiences has become more common
for Westerners. The desire to sample the exotic and experience the previously unknown, to be a traveller rather than a
tourist, has combined with improvements in air travel to
make it possible for a large number of people to journey to
destinations which would have been unthinkable for the
leisured artistocracy on their Grand Tours of the Northern
Mediterranean.

It is also suggested that the past 40 years have seen a clear
trend towards the commercialization of sex within the tourist
industry. Tourism has emerged out of an exploitative system
in which national images are manipulated by profit-seeking
companies for sale to pleasure-seeking customers (O'Grady
1980, p. 13). Many of the host nations exploit this and see
tourism as a vital component of national growth. The
message of the Thai Tourist Authority for instance is that
'Thailand, Asia's most exotic destination offers the visitor
many unique and unforgettable experiences'. It is also
recognized that some of these experiences will be sexual. A

remark made by the then Deputy Prime Minister of Thailand in November 1980 has been widely quoted in this context:

> I ask all governors to consider the natural scenery in your provinces, together with some forms of entertainment that some of you might consider disgusting and shameful because they are forms of sexual entertainment that attract tourists . . . We must do this because we have to consider the jobs that will be created for the people. (Perpignan 1981, p. 543)

It is because tourism provides 'jobs for the people' that it has always been an exploitative system. Almost from the start of its operations, Thomas Cook & Sons wielded enormous influence and power, forcing local guides to change their prices in Italy, exerting direct political influence in Egypt and acting as 'an agency for the consolidation of the [British] Empire' (Turner and Ash 1975, p. 58).

The ideological and economic effects of tourism on national image, which lead to attitudes like that of the Thai Minister quoted above, can be illustrated using the case of a small former English colony. Jamaica is the largest island in the Commonwealth Caribbean and attained independence in 1962. It is an exceptionally beautiful island, environmentally a true tropical paradise. Within the space of 4,411 square miles it is possible to find a variety of different natural environments from hot plains to high mountains, savannah country, tropical gulches and shell sand beaches. The heat of the midday sun is alleviated by sea breezes, making it an ideal holiday situation for tourists from Europe and North America. In 1980, a tourist poster for one of the newer resorts summed up the holiday image by exorting travellers to 'Pack up a bag and run away to Negril where you'll find 7 miles of deserted beach plus rum punch, lobsters and a hammock'.

The Jamaican tourist industry has been in existence for about 90 years. Until 1944, the island's main tourist function was as a stopover destination for cruise liners, but long-stay tourists began to arrive by air from North America after the

Second World War. This was the time when Ian Fleming, the author of the James Bond fantasy thrillers, whose house Golden Eye is now a tourist attraction, first settled on the north of the island. In the late 1970s there were between 70,000 and 80,000 visitors a year – temporary migrants to be added to the population of just under two million. Most visited during the high season, between December and April, and the overwhelming majority came not from England, but from North America (Jamaica Tourist Board 1978). This provided regular waged employment for some 10,000 people and income for others in craft manufacture and retailing. It also generated casual income for those who provide petty services to tourists: guides, escorts, gigolos and marijuana sellers. Yet, although tourism has increased Jamaica's foreign earnings, much of this income leaks abroad (Jefferson 1972, p. 177). This is not simply because tourism has developed on the principle of welcoming foreign investment, although foreign ownership represents just over half the hotel capacity, it is also because there is a high rate of import of both goods and foodstuffs in order to provide for tourist needs (pp. 177–8). These imports and the perceived life-style of tourists tend to raise local demand for foreign goods and, because of the higher prices charged to tourists, the cost of living in tourist areas also tends to rise.

The effect upon the labour market is not only to create jobs. Tourism raises the reserve price of labour and affects the stability of employment in other, lower-paid sectors. In addition, the tourist industry has its own inherent instability. Political disturbance and reports of civil disorder can severely affect tourist demand, as was the case during the 1976 and 1980 General Elections. Moreover, because of the seasonality of tourist arrivals, there are corresponding fluctuations in employment. Even spin-off employment in hotel and resort construction tends to be only temporary.

It is ironic that the temporary immigration of tourists is offset by the permanent outmigration of Jamaicans seeking a better life outside their welcoming island paradise (Taylor 1975; Government of Jamaica 1978). Jamaica and Jamaicans are represented to tourists as a packaged product, which is bought in thought before money changes hands for airline tickets. As Jamaican sociologist Taylor remarks, from the early days of tourism 'the portrait of the native and his environment was an "idyllic" one replete with waving palm trees and laughing men' (Taylor 1975, p. 19). Jamaicans are caught in the contradiction of being forced to endorse a mythical representation of their country and culture, at the same time as many of them are obliged to leave in order to seek a solution to their economic situation. The concrete result of all this is the geographical distribution of tourist enclaves. Luxury hotels cluster around attractive beaches, which have been appropriated for tourist use and are sometimes surrounded by guarded fences. Tourists are effectively discouraged from visiting nearby towns and villages, where largely unemployed Jamaicans may live in dwellings with no water, sanitation and electricity.

Those most firmly trapped in the contradiction are the Jamaicans employed in tourism. The work is relatively well-paid but depends on maintaining the myth and pleasing the tourist whatever the political and economic situation. Meanwhile tourists are bearers of another type of cultural image: the prosperous, modern way of life in what one Jamaican child described as 'the big shop called America' (comment recorded in Ennew Fieldnotes 1980). Tourists bring benefits and impart wealth, but only if Jamaicans submit to what Taylor calls the 'dehumanising' and 'demoralising' process of living up to a false image. Many tourists do complain – less about civil disturbance than about poor hotel service and constantly opportuning beggars in the streets. The latter is a reflex action derived from early tourism: 'fundamentally akin to the psychopathological sycophancy at the elite level with respect to persons and all things foreign' (Taylor 1975, p. 20). To a very large extent, Jamaicans have come to expect foreign investment and visitors to provide wealth, and have accepted the devaluation and manipulation of their culture which is the result of both old and new forms of imperialism. A Jamaican youth who makes seasonal forays to the north-coast holiday resorts in search of new clothes, jewellery and watches in return for being the companion of a 'lady tourist' is greeted with rueful admiration when he returns to his neighbourhood, where unemployment in the 17–25 age group may be as high as 60 per cent.

The inclusion of sexual pleasure in the relationship between foreign travel and enjoyment is not a recent phenomenon. Turner and Ash comment that 'during the nineteenth century, male prostitution catering largely for foreigners seems to have become something of an Italian speciality' (Turner and Ash 1975, p. 40). Goethe wrote with delight of the youths he saw on his Italian journey and of the easy availability of young people for the sexual pleasure of travellers (Goethe 1970, *passim*). The Grand Tour of Mediterranean countries was a classical mixture of the erotic and the exotic for many of his contemporaries. Latin countries also offered tourists 'direct release from the moral and physical restrictions of their countries of origin' (Turner and Ash 1975, p. 46). Goethe described himself as experiencing 'complete erotic freedom' for the first time in his life at the age of 40 during his visit to Rome.

Early explorers were also curious about the sexual mores of 'savage' societies. The first systematic ethnographic instructions for observing other cultures were given to François Péron, who accompanied a French expedition to the South Pacific in 1801. Péron was instructed to enquire if it were true that

> even in the most savage countries, the female sex preserves something of that sweet and secret power, rooted at once on her weakness, on her sensibility and on her charms
>
> [and]
>
> Are there in fact, any savage tribes so brutish that the women have absolutely no sense of modesty, that they completely lack inhibitions and that they go before men without a blush? (Degérando 1824 vol. 1, p. 89, my translation)

These were two of the few questions to which Péron provided a direct answer, reporting how disgusted he was at the appearance of naked aboriginal women in Australia, with the exception of a few in their mid-teens (Péron 1807–16, vol. 1, p. 252). His disgust seems to have been felt less at their lack of modesty than at their bodies, which did not accord with his preconceptions of female beauty. He failed to answer fully the other questions in the category of 'kinship', which included love, by which was meant sexual relations, and marriage, which was stated to be a characteristic of 'developing society' (Dégerando 1824, vol. 1, p. 89). The assumption in the eighteenth century, as for many twentieth century travellers, was that unregulated sexuality is typical of non-Western societies. Thus tourists to such places expect to enjoy a relaxation of the moral restrictions of their own culture: 'complete erotic freedom'.

It is within these types of structures that sexual tourism takes place, not as an aberration, but as part of normal international relations – economic, political and ideological. Preconceptions about sexual customs in other societies are not limited to the ethnic and racial stereotypes which have been discussed so far, but can be related to general ideas about foreigners. The dictionary definition of 'exotica' refers simply to anything which is not indigenous–things introduced from abroad which are both striking and attractive, appearing particularly colourful or unusual in contrast to the familiar world. What is different may not necessarily be regarded as attractive and exotic, it may appear disgusting and repulsive if it runs counter to particularly strong social prohibitions. Foodstuffs often fall into this category. Dogs, monkeys and guinea-pigs are forbidden food in England, raising expressions of disgust if they are discussed as edible, even though they are acceptable food in other countries. But this is relative to class and historical epoch. Frogs and snails, which used to have the same effect, are now acceptable to most middle-class diners. Similarly, Péron expressed disgust because Australian aboriginal women did not accord with his ideas of beauty, but the women of the South Pacific islands of Tahiti and

Hawaii have provided a stereotype of exotic beauty from Cook's first landfall. They were mythologized by Cook's artists, who presented them in the style of ancient Greece and Rome, and later by Gaugin, as the original sensual savages. At the time of first discovery, Cook was forced to make prohibitions against his sailors having sexual relations with local women, because the use of iron nails to smooth the transactions was threatening the structure of his ship (Wharton 1893, pp. 60–107).

Expected and approved behaviour at home similarly differs from conduct abroad. A particularly clear example of this is the contrast in home and abroad holiday features produced by the *Observer* magazine. In 1984, the magazine published a set of guides to the British holiday coastline in which entertainments and activities were typically described in terms of what a family with children might be expected to do. Margate, for instance is described as

> brash, candyfloss queen of the Thanet resorts . . . dominated by Bembon's big fairground wheel, sprouts hotels and amusement arcades, though Mr Derby keeps the traditions alive with his donkey rides on the beach. You can still see Turneresque sunsets, hear brass bands. Tidal pools now full of pedalos, canoes and bumper boats. Lost children rounded up in hut by clock tower where first aid given to dozens of fingers split in deck chairs. (*Observer* magazine 8 August 1984)

Entertainments more exciting than baby shows, yacht races and fruit machines are not mentioned.

This is not the case in a series of 'Insiders' Guides' to European cities, published in 1985 as a joint enterprise by the *Observer* and British Airways. Each substantial pull-out supplement contains a section on night-life, including explicit mention of prostitution. A photograph of 'street girls', one of whom has lifted her skirt to reveal her underwear to the camera, is included among 'Images of Lisbon', along with 'fishwives, in the market, butcher's assistant . . ., shoeshine men, itinerant peddler, city gent and nuptuals outside the

Quelez Palace.' The address of a 'seedy but safe' bar where prostitutes can be found is given in the text. The entry for 'Sexy Athens' is more explicit: 'Hotels and tour guides will do the procuring for you, but street soliciting is perfectly acceptable'. Warnings are given about pimps in a particular square, who are also pickpockets, along with directions to the areas frequented by transvestite and other homosexual prostututes. 'Sexy Vienna' is dismissed: 'compared to most European capitals, the city's erotic entertainment is on a fairly crude and primitive level', but a street where prostitutes can be found 'in large numbers' is named. Amsterdam meets with greater approval. Its 'Red Light' district 'has been a centre for prostitution for many centuries' and the women are 'a major tourist attraction'. Sex clubs and theatres are also named. Although West Berlin 'has no defined Red Light area', it is 'the centre for prostitution in Germany' and therefore warrants five photographs of description, which includes the following locations of street prostitution: 'centred on . . . Strasse and Strasse . . . with the latter having taken over from the Bahnhof Zoo as the tramping ground for the *Babystrich* – young heroin addicts of 12 years and up who find it the easiest way to support their habits. They are *not* licensed, and regard health checks as a joke' (all quotations from unpaginated *Insiders' Guides* to European Cities, published by the *Observer* magazine, various dates summer 1985, including essays by well-known writers and details of British Airways fares).

Seven years after 'Christiane F.' worked at the Bahnof Zoo there seems to be no change. Nor would one expect there to be. The biography of Michael Davidson, a self-confessed 'lover of little boys', has this to say about Berlin in the 1920s: 'one could if one were so disposed pursue little girls of 10 and 11, rouged and wearing short baby dresses, who promenaded from midnight to dawn in competition with lush blondes swathed in furs. There was also dartingly peripatetic sex-for-sale competition from doll-like little boys wearing lipstick, powder and eye shadow' (Davidson 1962, p. 150).

The actual situation produced by the relationship between

aesthetic standards, cultural expectations and economic dependency is often complex. There are clear differences in sexual preference which affect the extent to which minors are involved in sex tourism. Even though many groups in the developing world, which advocate the rights of homosexuals to practice in private, usually explicitly divorce themselves from movements for paedophilic rights, there are many indications that homosexual men are attracted to the idea of youth and romanticize young love. Whatever the case, sex tourism tends to emphasize the ready availability of young sexual partners in tourist resorts.

In 1973 a guide entitled *Where the Young Ones Are* was published in the United States, giving the male tourist information about the availability of child prostitutes in that country (Lloyd 1979). In the late 1970s and 1980s the *Spartacus* Gay Guides, published in the Netherlands, provided male homosexual tourists with up-to-date advice about the availability of sexual contacts in most countries. They publish specific advice about where to stay, where boys are available, how to make contact and how much to pay, as well as giving advice about the legal situation for homosexuals. The 1980 *Guide to Manila*, like other *Spartacus* guides, is similar in tone to the *Observer*/British Airways Guides, as the following quotation reveals:

> If you enter Harrison Plaza Manila at the entrance nearest to Century Park Sheraton you will come immediately into an area which has roller skating, bump cars and gaming machines. There are usually several hundred boys available at one time in that area. It is open from ten in the morning until ten at night. It is rather similar to a fish market in terms of business and haggling over prices and you may prefer the rather more relaxed situation of the VIP restaurant at the central point of the complex. (Spartacus 1980)

Spartacus is published in Amsterdam by John D. Stamford, who apparently boasts that he has personally sampled many of the boys he recommends, and that part of his service

includes offering tourists the personal assistance of boys
employed as Spartacus guides in each of the countries
covered in the portfolios (Kaiser 1981, p. 2). In effect, these
boys act as pimps, liaising between the tourist and the local
market:

> JUNE. Born 5th October, 1963. An experienced call-
> boy who has so far been very good with our clients but
> has recently begun to deteriorate. Some complaints
> about him asking too much and turning up in somewhat
> effeminate dress have made him slightly less attractive.
> Paedophiles would perhaps be particularly interested to
> meet June because he sometimes is able to bring his
> much younger cousin, who is also his 'apprentice'.
> (Spartacus 1980, Part II, p. 1)

In a press conference recorded by *Terre des Hommes*, the
development expert Tim Bond claimed that in Sri Lanka
numerous boys prostitute themselves in tourist areas. Bond
estimated that there are about 2,000 boys between the ages
of 7 and 17 who work in this way, many of whom are also
involved in making pornographic films. Some of the boys
Bond talked to came from disrupted homes and were living
independent of kin, but there were others who lived with their
families, continued to attend school and only prostituted
themselves on a casual basis. Boy prostitutes in Sri Lanka
work independently, and are not controlled by either pimps
or brothels, but the time in which they can rely upon remaining in this trade is limited. By late adolescence they have
already lost their market value for tourists who seek younger
partners than they can usually find in their countries of origin
(Bond 1981).

In recent years there have been many reports of sex tourism
in the South East Asian countries of Thailand, South Korea
and the Philippines (Perpignan 1981 and 1983; Manazan
1982; *Esclavage* 1981; Moselina 1978, Matsui 1980; *ISIS* 1979
and 1984). Package holidays are arranged for heterosexual
tourists through travel agents in the developed world, such as
the 'Rosie Reisen' agency of West Germany (ISIS Inter-

national Bulletin no. 13, 1979). Sexual experience is an explicit part of the package, indeed it may be the only object of the journey. A brochure published in the Netherlands, acquired by concerned Asian women during their protest against sex tours organized in Europe, begins: 'if you ever want to have an exclusive and special sex holiday, which you will remember for the rest of your life, then this is a unique chance in your life . . .' (in Barry et al. 1984, p. 123). Where other travel agencies might offer coach tours to historical and archaeological sites, or the pleasures of natural scenery, sex tour agencies advertize transport to plentiful brothels and bars, as well as hotel based services. Even agencies which offer a broader range of activities and attractions still cater for the single male tourist.

> Night Life Special
> For those seeking night life in Bangkok we offer the . . . Hotel. The hotel offers swimming pool, gardens, coffee shop. Rooms are simply furnished with bath, shower and balcony. Definitely not for families, but batchelors seem to rate it highly. (Kuoni's *Worldwide* brochure, current from December 1983 to December 1984)

The hotel in question was described in a television documentary *The Road to Hualonpong* as providing a customer service for the treatment of sexually transmitted diseases.

Tourists who take advantage of sex package holidays travel from all over Western Europe, the United States, Australasia and Japan. Out of a total of 236,350 Japanese tourists visiting the Philippines in 1979, 90 per cent were male (Asian Women's Liberation 1984). Reports suggest that sex tourism in South East Asia is so ubiquitous that all tourists, regardless of sex or gender, are assumed to require sexual services during their stay in the larger hotels of Bangkok, Manila or Seoul. The widely available *All Asia Guide*, which is aimed at the travelling businessman, also implicitly makes the assumption that business will be combined with sexual pleasures: 'Bangkok's famous bars . . . continue to delight, chiefly on account of the bar girls . . . It can be arranged to have one of the girls accompany you to your hotel – just how friendly the action remains can depend on the flow of funds' (*All Asia Guide* 1984; Far Eastern Economic Review Ltd., p. 513).

In South Korea, many prostitutes are attached to a type of restaurant known as Kinsaeng House, which is very popular among the predominantly Japanese male tourists. There are about 5,000 of these houses, many of which are recognized by the government, while others operate clandestinely. Women who are officially recognized and licensed by the Kinsaeng House section of the Korean Association for International Tourism are supposed to be educated to high school level and are given a general culture course before receiving their health licences. It has been suggested that the 'culture' taught is anti-communism and sex education. At the end of their training they are issued with identification cards which also allow them free access to tourist hotels, as well as free movement at night during times of curfew (*ISIS* 1979, pp. 6–8; *Asian Women's Federation* 1980, pp. 11–14).

There have been campaigns against the sexual exploitation of Asian women in sex tourism. Women's groups throughout the world have protested at airports where sex tourists are known to embark and land, calling the flights involved 'Gonorrhoea Expresses', and greeting the passengers with heckling and derision (*ISIS* 1981, Davidson 1982). This type of pressure has encouraged firms to offer family holidays as rewards for service, rather than batchelor trips abroad as they did previously. The face of sex tourism has changed a little. Until 1980 it was common for groups of up to 200 Japanese males to visit the Philippines, for example, for three days of sexual pleasure. But synchronized protests during the visit of the Japanese Prime Minister to ASEAN countries in January 1981 took effect. Japan Airlines has had to cancel two of its daily flights to Manila, and hotel occupancy has decreased. Holiday advertisements in Japanese outlets have changed from showing near-naked females to pictures of landscapes. But prostitution remains, and the customers are still largely Japanese. The difference is that disguised traffic in Philippino women to Japan has increased (Perpignan 1983, pp. 12–13).

The main stimulus for sex tourism comes from customer demand. It is clear that sex tourism in South East Asia has escalated because of United States military imperialism and Japanese economic aggression. United States military presence in the Philippines dates back to 1904, but the first real expansion in sex tourism came in the 1950s during the Korean war, with military personnel seeking rest and recreation during leave periods, and special centres being built to cater for their leisure requirements. Sexual services seem to be regarded as a necessary part of recreation by United States military personnel, due, no doubt, to a 'male incontinence' theory of sexuality. Local economies responded rapidly to the ready injection of dollars. As the Vietnam war followed fast upon the conflict in Korea, 'comfort girls' and 'recreation' continued to be supplied for the soldiers in areas around military bases or designated recreation areas (*Balai* vol. II no. 4, pp. 21–2; Asian Women's Liberation 1984, no. 6, pp. 4–12). These centres were built mainly during the Vietnam war for soldiers to use in Vietnam, Thailand, the Philippines, Korea and Taiwan. When the war ended, prostitution in Vietnamese bases ceased; but the 7th Fleet's home port is still Subic Naval Base, and together with Clark Air Base it forms the largest concentration of United States troops in foreign territory. The rest and recreation centre in Olangapo in the Philippines remains the largest base for prostitution in Asia. A total of 7,000 hospitality girls and prostitutes are licensed by the city in return for weekly medical checks (Matsui in Asian Women's Liberation 1980, p. 5–7). In Thailand, the military bases have declined and the remaining prostitutes cater for Thai military personnel or Japanese tourists. The main centre for sex tourism has shifted to Pattaya Beach, which is used by Midway troops when they are in port (p. 7).

Japanese economic prosperity arose because of the emergency demands of both Korean and Vietnamese wars. Economic expansion into the surrounding areas began with foreign investment in the early 1970s. The strategy has changed from a focus on manufacturing to large-scale projects which exploit natural resources. Tourism is thus part of a general economic expansion; Japanese businessmen now seek rest and relaxation from the stresses of competitive business in the same way that soldiers used to seek rest away from the battlefield (Asian Women's Liberation 1980, p. 8; Perpignan 1983, p. 12; Moselina 1978; Manazan 1982; O'Grady 1980, pp. 16–18). Tourism has become too important to national economies for governments to take ready action against prostitution. In Thailand, for instance, tourism is the third largest component of the GNP, in the Philippines it is the fourth. But, just as prostitutes benefit least from the trade in their sexuality, so the host nations in the tourist industry are the last to gain profits from the trade in their national culture.

Whether it is the *Spartacus* guide catering for the paedophile tourist, or the many advertisements appearing in the press in developed countries encouraging heterosexual males to enjoy the delights of submissive Asian girls, tourists and agencies alike often use the myth that there is no harm involved because the culture of the host country entails a greater sexual freedom than that enjoyed in the tourist's homeland. The actual sexual morality of the host countries is ignored. What is conveniently viewed instead is an apparent freedom, created by the demands of the tourist customers. In a mutual exchange of dreams, the tourist finds the exotic promiscuity of Sri Lanka, Seoul or Bangkok, while the prostitutes come into contact with the bountiful, prosperous developed world.

There is little evidence for making a specific link between sex tourism and child prostitution. Many prostitutes catering for tourists are under the age of 18, and many may be under 16, yet it seems that, even in the case of boy prostitutes, few are pre-pubertal. One universal feature of prostitution is that it is a trade in which success is determined by youth above many other factors. What is being sold is not just sexuality, but youthful sexuality. An old prostitute is a redundant prostitute, as Tim Bond pointed out in the case of Sri Lankan boys, and as Peruvian prostitutes found out in Callao.

Because youth and physical attractiveness are for sale alongside sexuality, it follows that higher prices will be paid for younger and more attractive prostitutes (Perpignan 1983). In almost all cases, tourists to developing countries have more available cash for these commodities than local buyers have. This is partly because they come from more wealthy nations and partly because they are on holiday, with normal rules for saving and spending suspended. This relaxation of standards is also likely to apply to sexual mores. At least two studies have suggested that men are more likely to sample sexual activities with children, or give way to repressed paedophilic tendencies, while away from home. Not only does the fact of being on holiday give the individual greater licence, but also the rules of another society do not have so great a deterrent effect as those in which one was socialized (Rossman 1979; Perpignan 1983). This culture effect is probably exacerbated by the fact of being among people who are racially different. The 50 clients interviewed by researchers in the Philippines reported negative feelings about aggressive women of their own race or culture and positive feelings about passive Philippino women (Perpignan 1983).

The alternative to the tourist trade, in which the rich travel to visit and view the poor, is a traffic in human beings which brings or attracts the poor to serve the rich. This is related to migrations of people from tourist areas, like Jamaica, in search of better jobs and working conditions, and to the presence of large 'guestworker' populations doing low-paid work in prosperous nations like West Germany. There have been suggestions from various sources that a modern equivalent of the 'white slave trade' exists, to move women and children in large numbers across national borders (Fernand-Laurent 1983).

Runaway minors in any country are particularly vulnerable to exploitation by non-related adults and could become the subject of traffic. The 1949 Convention on prostitution also relates to the traffic in persons, particularly traffic across national boundaries. There are two main areas of concern, although there is little detailed information available. The first involves hiring a woman or girl with a view to making her engage in prostitution in any country, state or territory other than that in which she usually lives. Some circumstantial evidence indicates that women and girls are supplied along recognized routes (Karunatilleke 1981; INTERPOL 1975, published as an annex to Barry 1979).

> According to this incomplete information, few regions and few countries, (with the possible exception of those with highly planned economies) are free of the international traffic in women, and that traffic is far from being confined to a flow from South (less developed) to North (developed): it would be more accurate to say that the movement involves the traffic of poor women towards rich men in all directions. (Fernand-Laurent 1983, p. 12)

The second form is known as 'disguised traffic' and involves hiring women or girls to work away from their homes in the entertainment industry, in such jobs as dancing, cabaret performance and bar work, in which they will be likely to come into contact with prostitutes and pimps and may become involved themselves. It is argued that many women who take up this kind of employment know that they will be expected to prostitute themselves. This does not alter the fact that there may also be many who are ignorant of these extra conditions and are attracted by the idea of legitimate, and possibly glamourous employment (Ohse 1984, p. 45).

Women may be coerced into prostitution by being forced to repay debts to the employment agency which paid their ticket to another country and found them employment. Their passports may be confiscated until the debt is repaid and they may be threatened with exposure to immigration authorities if they try to break away from their employment. They are strangers in a foreign land and alien culture and do not understand what rights they have. Furthermore, the journey they make to the developed world is founded on a dream of making a better life than they had in their poverty-stricken homeland; this is a hard dream to abandon. Some women who know they are likely to be exploited in the labour market of their own country may consider prostitution in a foreign land a more pleasant alternative, and hope to return home relatively wealthy as a result (Ohse 1984 *passim*).

The ideal of a compliant, faithful and passive woman from an exotic culture, which clients of Philippino prostitutes described to researchers, has probably been instrumental in the development of a further traffic in women, organized by bureaux which arrange marriages between men in the developed world and females from developing countries (Ohse 1984, Part 2b). This might be regarded as another kind of disguised traffic – sexual services are being transferred for a cash payment, although this is on a permanent basis, and other services like domestic work and reproduction are also part of the transaction. In addition, the male client offers not just a single payment but permanent support and protection. Nevertheless, the marriage bureau business shows some of the racist characteristics which are found in sex tourism and also reveals a tendency towards dishonest trading (Claire and Cottingham 1984).

Most of the women recruited by the bureaux travel from South East Asia, but others come from Africa and South America. It appears to be a profitable business for agencies based in Europe and the United States. In a recent book on international trafficking in women, Ulla Ohse draws attention to an official enquiry into an international marriage travel agency known as Menger's Travels. The enquiry alleged that fraud, traffic in persons, and the promotion of prostitution had taken place. The agency operated in West Germany and advertized the delights of 'gentle, tender and faithful' girls from Thailand, Taiwan and the Philippines (Ohse 1984, p. 15). The agency guaranteed marriage within a year for the West German clients. Clients of the German Interpart Company, which offered the same kind of services, chose the girls of their dreams from a catalogue of photographs and were reputed to pay the bureau 9,000 marks (US$5,000) for a return ticket to Bangkok with accommodation in a hotel in order to visit their future wives. If a marriage were arranged, a further 3,000 marks had to be paid to the company (p. 13). The girls and women who seek husbands in this way do not necessarily find happiness. In some cases they also have to pay a fee to the bureaux. Some women arrive in Europe to find that their promised spouse does not exist. The bureaux then offer work (often in the entertainment industry) which may be destined to lead the girls into prostitution (Ohse 1984 *passim*).

Not all females involved in prostitution through disguised traffic are under 18 years of age. But one kind of traffic in children is reputed to specialize in young children. The evidence that children who have disappeared from developing countries are sold in Europe and the United States for the explicit purpose of prostitution and pornography is scant. Most has been gathered by the French lawyer Renee Bridel, but the sources are almost always sensational newspaper reports. Bridel alleges that children are either bought from desparate, impoverished parents by false adopters who offer a better life abroad, or kidnapped and sold to middle men who ship them abroad (Bridel 1982). A typical report is that in which a Bolivian lawyer was accused of having bought a boy from kidnappers for 22,000 pesos (US$40) and sold him to a Belgian couple for US$10,000 (*Revue Internationale de l'Enfant* 1984, no. 61). Such cases occur frequently in the press and it is claimed that adoption rings and aid agencies operate as covers for this traffic (McCall n/d; Ennew 1982). One report suggested that officials of an agency offering relief in refugee camps in Bangladesh are in fact involved in trafficking in unaccompanied refugee children (McCall n/d). But evidence of these children being found in prostitution or pornography in the developed world or elsewhere is far from conclusive.

6

Pornography

There are always definitional problems for any discussion of pornography. Debates are complicated by assertions of artistic or literary merit as well as by moral arguments. My purpose here is not just to examine the worldwide extent of child pornography, but also to discuss its relationship to other forms of pornography and representations of children in general. For that reason I am adopting a definition of pornography as the representation of sex and/or sexuality – in literature or in visual media such as drawings, sculptures, photographs, films and video – for the sole purpose of stimulating the viewer. Such representations display the human body with the single explicit aim of arousing sexual desire and/or providing or provoking sexual gratification. The images may be of an individual, or a group, clothed or naked, with or without animals or inanimate objects (see also Williams Report 1979, paragraph 8.2, p. 103). Pornographic representations are used by the beholder to stimulate and/or assuage sexual desire. They reduce the depicted person or persons to dehumanized and desocialized sexual objects in the eye of the beholder. Pornography trivializes sexual relationships by separating them from social life. It establishes an imbalanced power relationship between the portrayed and the viewing subject (Dworkin 1981, Williams Report 1979).

It is difficult to draw a line between pornography and erotica. Indeed I sometimes wonder if it is legitimate to do so. The general argument is that the erotic is never unitary in its representation; it is not solely concerned with sexuality. Although the erotic represents the sexual, it also provides distraction in the form of extra subject matter or aesthetic considerations. Yet the distinction between the erotic and the pornographic is seldom clear, and many representations which would be defined as erotic by their creators can be viewed as pornographic by an observer. This is often a matter of either individual or cultural evaluation. In some societies the depiction of any kind of sexuality may be considered pornographic; in others almost any representation is allowable. Moreover, seemingly innocent representations may become pornographic in other contexts – the meaning changes according to the way in which they are used. Thus a picture of a naked, smiling child might originate as a portrayal of familial affection and childish innocence, but it could be rendered pornographic by its inclusion in a magazine containing pictures which display explicit sexual acts. In this way, even the 'innocently childlike' qualities portrayed in the photograph become the objects of sexual desire, as in the paedophile's search for a lost childhood. This is also an example of the way in which pornography may depict as 'sexual' subjects which are not generally imbued with associations of sexual desire or active sexuality. Thus the context of a representation may be as important as the content in determining whether or not it is pornographic. In the same way, there is no necessary connection between pornography and material gain, for pornographic material is frequently produced for private use (Tyler 1982, p. 9). Nor is the intention of the producer of an image a primary indication of its pornographic nature. In the wide range of sexual tastes and individual fixations, almost any image may be seized upon to stimulate sexual desire (Catholic Social Welfare Commission 1977, p. 3).

The child pornography about which recent concern has been expressed is largely the visual rather than written forms of pornography, because of the relatively more important effects for children. Pornographic representations in literature stimulate through fantasy and the imagination. They may incite adults to commit sexual acts with children, and thus may have a corrupting function; they may be used to introduce children to sexual activities with adults; but visual representations, particularly photographs, have a more immediate impact. The acts portrayed may be real or simulated, but in both cases they are portrayals of actual things happening to actual people. This can give a false appearance of 'normality' when used to introduce children to the idea of sexual activities (Tyler 1982, p. 11). But pornography depicting adult sexual acts with children cannot be produced without an act taking place which is defined as illegal in almost all countries of the world (Tyler 1982, pp. 4 and 9; Illinois Legislative Investigating Commission 1980 pp. 27 and 30).

This is why any justification for the existence of child pornography is invalid. Justifications take the form of arguments that pornography is a safety valve or harmless representation of aspects of sexuality which in spite of, or perhaps because of, their social devaluation by the majority hold an attraction for, and act as a stimulation to, a minority. By this argument, pornography allows people to indulge in their fantasies without encouraging them to act upon them (Constantine 1979, p. 506). These assertions founder on the fact that some form of real or simulated act must have taken place for photographic representations to exist. In addition, there is a message about power implicit in all pornography, particularly that involving children. This imbalance may also be extended to fantasies about actual physical domination. The argument in favour of pornography would suggest that the depiction of acts which relate violence to sexuality does not encourage actual violent behaviour in people exposed to the representations, but allows them to deal in a passive way with their own latent or acknowledged violence, which thus never becomes manifest. Some studies have attempted to prove that imprisoned sex offenders may be people who have had less exposure to pornography during their lives than non offenders (e.g. Thornberry and Silverman 1971; Schultz 1980, chapter 19). But these studies are not conclusive, and the argument is as vacuous as the general defence of pornography. An act of violence, real or simulated, against a child must first have taken place for the photograph, film or video to exist.

While laws against the production and distribution of pornography exist in many countries, legislation is always faced with the problem of definition. In countries where the freedom of the press and the individual are highly valued, both the recognition of pornographic material and legislation against it become even more complex (*Ideas Forum* no. 16, p. 9). Some countries, like Hong Kong and Mexico, make no distinction between old and young, male and female, but simply prohibit all forms of pornography, although this does not mean that no pornography is available. Under the law of England and Wales the definition of pornography depends largely on the interpretation of the terms 'obscene' and 'indecent'. There are further problems in most countries which make distinctions between the artistic, erotic depiction of sexual acts, and the obscene or indecent depiction of the same acts. Nevertheless, there seems to be some general agreement about the negative or pornographic connotations of specific sexual acts, such as bestiality and adult–child sexual activities. Thus the photographic depiction of a sexual act between an adult and a child (however 'child' may be defined) tends to be regarded as pornographic because it involves a child, rather than because it involves a depiction of any particular activity.

The simplest legislation sanctions the producer of the image, rather than the person(s) performing the act (Government of Canada 1984, p. 59), but the legislation tends to be formulated under measures for the protection of children, rather than within the framework for legislation about pornography in general. The 1978 Protection of Children Act of England and Wales, for instance, makes it an offence for a person or body to take or permit to be taken indecent photographs of children under 16, to show or distribute these, or to publish or advertise them. Photography in this case includes all films and videos. This is why many easily available United Kingdom sex magazines print disclaimers such as: 'We do not promote or condone certain activities which are unlawful or could be harmful; such as underage sex, incest, bestiality, necrophilia' or claim that all their models are professional models and over 18 years of age: 'The content of this material is sexually explicit, having educational value in its use by adults in the privacy of their own homes. All models are professionals and at least 18 years of age.' This last quotation concerns homosexual material, with some models clearly pre-pubertal. Models over 18 may look younger of course, and many young prostitutes who pose for pornography have false papers provided by their pimps. Models over 18 are often portrayed as children in various scenarios and costumes. Thus an advertisement for a film called *School for Sex* states: 'The ageing headmaster extracts his sexual pleasure (both intercourse and oral). Full Costumes, headmaster's robes and gymslips', and a book advertisement reads: 'Young girls displaying their awareness of their developing womanhood. Really high quality shots of these delightful darlings in action.'

Although many of these images actually show adults dressed as children, minors do appear in many different forms of photographic representation catering for both homosexual and heterosexual markets, for paedophiles are as likely to be bisexual or heterosexual as they are to be homosexual. Moreover, the fantasy element in photographs like those taken by Charles Dodgson (Lewis Carroll) of the child 'Alice' in the late-nineteenth century have their parallels in the range of child pornographic photographs now available. Pornography achieves its effects of stimulating desire by objectification and by fantasy. The former is a 'short cut to desire' which ignores the individual person in favour of representations of the body or parts of the body:

What makes pornography recognizable are its *non*-transparent features, the elements which constitute it as a distinctive representational genre – a certain rhetoric of the body, forms of narration, placing and wording of captions and titles, stylisations and postures, a repertoire of milieux and costumes, lighting techniques etc. (Brown 1981, pp. 6–7)

Thus there is a limited range of textual motifs which appear in the type of pornography which emphasizes youth or children. These include such elements as the idea that the desire of young people is greater than that of the mature person, and that young females can be aggressive pleasure-seekers. Thus 'nymphomaniac' is a recurrent term, as are 'enjoy' and 'action'. Another element which frequently occurs is reference to large penis size. This is a feature in adult pornography also, but the emphasis in that case is on the extraordinary individual. In child pornography, even the average penis can be thought of as large in relation to the immature genitals of children, and fingers or thumbs may be used as penis substitutes in the representations. Yet another motif is that of the adult as voyeur of acts of juvenile mutual exploration or masturbation, including oral and anal sexual acts, with particular emphasis upon viewing ejaculation. Accompanying texts often draw the observer's attention to the sexual energy of youth.

Many reports on child pornography limit themselves to statements intended to shock and are thus prurient themselves. I find it unhelpful to be told that 'For forty-five dollars one can purchase a film in living color and see a nine-year-old getting fucked by two Arab boys, then by an adult' (Rush 1980, p. 79). This evidence is not only non-specific, it also uses emotive language. There is no need to do this, for the material speaks for itself. The following is a brief description of the contents of a small booklet of black and white photographs of child pornography. The book is in a series obtainable by mail order from an address in Denmark. It is advertised as showing 'White pre-teen girls in Action' and claims to show 'photographs imported from the USA'.

Cover: Girl of about two years old sitting with genitals exposed, and an adult finger inserted into her vagina; adult not visible except finger.
  1 Small-breasted, possibly pre-teen girl lying across a

bed unclothed. Adult presence indicated only by an erect penis.

2 Pre-pubertal female genitals, with no pubic hair, spread in front of camera; the only other element is a hand, which could be a child's, inserting a dildo.

3 Some line drawings of adults and children, nineteenth-century, classroom motif, in a style derivative of Hogarth.

4 Pre-teen naked couple about to copulate, female above.

5 Two small naked girls with their bodies only shown.

6 Two small girls and a small boy, naked as in 5, simply facing the camera.

7 A naked girl, aged about eight or nine, no obvious sexual connotation except nudity.

8 Two naked girls, with fingers placed artificially as if for acts of mutual masturbation. Simply lying in front of the camera.

9 A girl of about six years old, dressed only in a pair of knickers, with her hand over her crotch.

10 Faceless man apparently penetrating pre-pubertal girl. Her face is visible and contorted in what could be pain or orgasm.

11 Two little girls naked with their genitals exposed, not touching each other.

12 A clothed girl of about six lifts her skirt to show her knickers.

13 A toddler lifts her dress up, and looks at a (male?) thumb on her naked genitals.

14 A facsmile of many *Playboy* images. A little girl lies back with her dress held up to expose her genitals with a dildo partially inserted. Her eyes are half-closed and her expression is content.

15 and 16 Three naked girls in the open air, the second photograph looks as if it were taken on a family picnic. No sexual connotation apart from nudity.

17 The girl in picture 12, this time holding the crotch of her knickers aside to expose her genitals.

18 Once again the *Playboy* facsimile, but this time with a girl of eight to ten years old.

19 A naked little girl crouching with her genitals spread wide towards the camera.

20 A very pretty girl of about eight, with a 'knowing' expression, sitting cross-legged, dressed only in a T-shirt, so that her genitals are exposed.

21 A little girl being straddled by a man, with his penis in her mouth, while another person (possibly child or youth) performs cunnilingus on her.

22 A little girl, naked and with unpleasant scabs on her legs, lies spreadeagled with her genitals and anus exposed, no face visible.

23 A naked female baby, lying with its legs in the air. Could be a family snapshot.

24 A thin, pre-pubertal girl bent forwards over a bed, wearing stockings. A man holds her down with one hand on her back and another on her right thigh, his penis inserted in her vagina.

25 Standing girl with immature breasts apparently enjoying cunnilingus from a kneeling boy.

26 Small girl sitting astride the legs of a man with an erect penis, her genitals exposed (an image repeated from one of the drawings above).

27 Naked pre-pubertal girls standing; holding signs saying 'fuck' and 'me'.

Other titles in the same series are advertised on the final page. It is clear that they feature many of the same models. Such titles include exotic models ('from Bangkok') and homosexual material ('mini-boys'). The objectification typical of pornography is seen in the way that nearly one third of the pictures show only parts of bodies, or faceless bodies. The same child is used in more than one picture and, judging by the quality, many pictures are of amateur origin. About half are professional standard. On the evidence of this magazine, and other material, it seems unlikely that there are many children involved. Moreover, as is common in speciality pornography, the style of clothing and background indicate that some of these pictures have not been taken in the past four decades. Five out of the total twenty-eight images could be family photographs and would have no necessary sexual context if they did not appear in this magazine. In the case of picture 12, I have an almost identical snapshot of a neighbour's child which I took playfully at a family barbecue. At the time her parents joked that I could blackmail her with it when she was older. The picture of the baby on page 23 is not unlike the photograph used to advertise babycare equipment which I have included in figure 4, the 'knowing expression' of the girl on page 20 is similar to that depicted on a recent cover of a woman's magazine, and many of the photographs in this booklet are no different to the little girl wrapped in a towel used to advertise home insurance (figure 4). Less than two-thirds of the images have an explicit sexual connotation and could stand alone as examples of child pornography.

I do not subscribe to the view that large numbers of children are involved in child pornography. The same children, often obviously filmed or photographed in a single session, are shown in more than one product of the pornographic media (Tyler 1982, p. 10). The mixture, particularly where pre-pubertal children or infants are involved, is often non-generic. The pictures are just pictures of children and young people, and the sexual connotations of what might be regarded as purely innocent pictures are only achieved by the contiguity of other obviously sexual images, which may be drawings rather than photographs. The pictures are generally of poor quality and strive after effect (Gersen 1979). Advertising copy often stresses that the quality of the product is 'excellent' and 'new', indicating the significance of amateur and well-used products on this market (Illinois Legislative Investigating Commission 1980, p. 27).

The term 'blue movies' was first applied to pornographic films because of the poor quality or reproduction. Advances in technology have made a difference. Videos, for instance, do not have to be sent away for the film to be developed, so that there is less danger of detection and prosecution. It is

Figure 4 Three Common Images of Childhood.
Note: These images are often used in advertisements. While there may be justification for demonstrating a disposable nappy on a real baby, the positioning of the adult hand could be a factor in stimulating paedophile fantasy (see chapter 7). The expression on the faces of both little girls is only arguably innocent. And is there really a connection between a girl dressed only in a towel and household insurance?

now both cheap and easy for amateurs to produce good reproductive quality films (Tyler 1982, p. 7; Schultz 1980, p. 273). Films made for private use sometimes only enter the commercial market after prior circulation among a group of people with similar tastes, such as paedophiles, who may be in touch only by post (Tyler 1982, p. 5). The child pornography which is found on national and international markets has its source in both amateur and professional circles, and it is by no means clear that there is a vast, highly profitable industry involved. Nevertheless it is clear that the professional film-makers who are involved also produce 'soft' pornography and sometimes more reputable products.

Children who become involved in pornography do so in a variety of ways. They usually receive no payment for their participation in the products of the amateur photographer or film-maker. Force is seldom used, and children are gradually drawn into the activity by an adult whom they have come to trust. The following case is typical. A male public-sector employee, who lived alone in an apartment on a large housing estate in the Parisian suburb, made friends with several neighbouring families. This resulted in invitations to the young sons, aged between nine and twelve years, to visit him in his apartment. Once friendly relations had been established in the course of several visits, he dared the boys to lower their trousers. As the game progressed with further dares, the man was able to take photographs. After a time, the sister of one of the boys became disturbed by changes in his personality and alerted other adults (*Femme et Monde* 1982, no. 57). The gradual involvement in sexual activities means that no force is necessary in order to obtain the children's participation. Their shame at performing acts which they vaguely perceive as wrong ensures their silence.

Study of the available child pornography suggests that some pictures of pre-pubertal children and infants may be taken by parents in the home. Some of the acts involved appear to be more simulated than real, and this distancing may provide the mechanism by which children were willing to take part: the events are not happening to their real selves

(SOS Enfants 1981). Children have been known to excuse their participation on the grounds that they have never actually taken part in sexual intercourse in front of a camera: 'I posed for months and still remained a virgin, I was doing a job, I wasn't involved' (SOS Enfants 1981, my translation). But this is not sufficient to justify their use in such depictions or to claim that no harm is done to them. The representations of the child's sexuality exist independently of him or her and are thus alienating, particularly if the depictions become commodities to be bought and sold. Thus there is a chance that the child may at a later date be confronted by this objectified representation of his or her sexuality, which could be experienced as a threat to personal integrity (Government of Canada 1984, p. 54).

In the professional sphere, child pornography is a relatively lucrative commodity, and children may well find that they are able to earn more from allowing themselves to be photographed or filmed than from prostitution. The organization SOS Enfants reports that children may earn up to 50,000 francs for three days' filming (SOS Enfants 1981). Even so, compared with the money that the film might earn for producers and distributors, the child's payment may be relatively slight. Contrary to supposition, prices of child pornography are not that much higher than those of adult pornography. In one Dutch brochure, eight out of twenty-three listed items priced between £7 and £49 for the UK market were child pornography. The four books were £7–8 each, the video £49 and the films £30–33 each. Higher prices were clearly asked for acts of anal and oral intercourse or for special features like bestiality, and this appears to be as important a factor as age in determining price, as in the case of prostitution.

The films and magazines in which children appear are easily available to a variety of consumers. Although there are legal obstacles in many countries, and in international trade, for the distributors of child pornography, it has been claimed in at least one study that it is easy to go into a sex shop and buy child pornography (SOS Enfants 1981). Research for this book showed that the price of child pornography may be from double to ten times the price of adult heterosexual pornography, according to the country in which it is marketed and the type of image sold. The price of pictures of intergenerational sexual acts is higher than pictures of naked children, and age is another factor in pricing. It is usually fairly easy to obtain in shops and particularly easy to track down by following up mail order advertisements in 'soft' pornography outlets, or even in national newspapers (figure 5). In urban areas of the United Kingdom speciality pornography is often available in the back rooms of sex shops, or on special request by customers. In other countries, like the Netherlands, where restrictions are non-existent or lax, child pornography is freely and openly available in shops. A further source of distribution is mail order. Advertisements appear in adult leisure magazines, or magazines with pornogaphic material in which adults are depicted (sometimes dressed as children), for books, films and videos featuring 'the very young' or 'schoolgirls'. Other advertisements are coded to avoid detection.

There is no concrete evidence that the production of child pornographic material is increasing at epidemic rates. As with adult pornography, particularly the more extraordinary kind, many sequences and stills are used over and over again in different outlets (Tyler 1982, pp. 9–10). It is clear from the quality of print or costumes and style that many child depictions are up to fifty years old. Magazines and distribution companies are short-lived and material is thus reproduced monotonously. But the customer is in no position to complain to consumer councils if he or she is dissatisfied with the product. Toby Tyler, who is a United States Police expert in child sexual exploitation, suggests that there are likely to be few large-scale organizations involved in the production of child pornography, and most is likely to be produced by individuals or groups of paedophiles (Tyler 1982, p. 5).

Nevertheless there have been suggestions that children are being bought and sold for use in the pornography industry (Bridel 1982). It is stated that children, often from the developing world, are kidnapped or collected from the streets

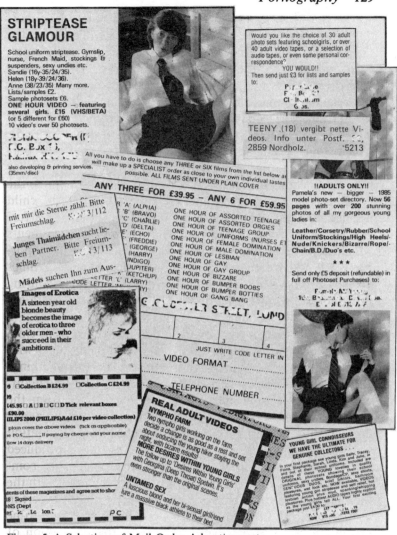

Figure 5 A Selection of Mail Order Advertisements.
Note: These are from magazines which are available in high street newsagents in the United Kingdom and West Germany. More explicit material can be obtained from magazines available through more obscure retail outlets.

where they live and used in the more extreme videos and 'snuff movies'. In these a child or woman is subjected to sexual indignities and finally killed. Snuff movies undoubtedly exist and the action is not always simulated. This genre of film corresponds to a cultural trend which is widespread and has regular commercial outlets in cinemas and as videos. One of the clearest examples is the film *Cannibal Holocaust*, which is popular and widely distributed and depicts a group of male and female anthropologists being tortured, subjected to sexual indignities and eventually killed by an Amazonian tribe. It is claimed that this is a film of actual events, which resulted from the anthropologists' camera being left running accidentally. The emphasis in the film is on sexual aspects, as can be seen from advertisements for *Cannibal Holocaust* which depict a woman impaled vaginally and orally. Snuff films are perhaps the most exotic and thus expensive of all visual pornographic representations; but although they are profitable, the market for them is likely to be limited. They are not easily available nor, so far as I have been able to establish, are there a great many in this genre. It is difficult to say for certain whether 'snuff movies' represent a few isolated instances or a growing trend. But it seems likely that children who become involved in these representations are either promised large sums of money or goods, or forced to perform under threats of physical violence. Whatever the case, it draws attention to the fact that coercion may be used to ensure children's participation, and this is an extreme example of the way in which sexuality is treated as a market commodity. In snuff movies it is not just sexuality but also the individual's life which is a commodity.

A recent case in California drew attention to the coercion aspect of child pornography. Kindergarten children were allegedly forced into participation, with the entire staff implicated in the events (Kaplan 1984, p. 91). The children, all under the age of six, were threatened with physical danger and even death if they did not take part. It was alleged that they were shown animals being killed and told that they would die in the same way if they informed their parents. The alleged offences only came to light when parents investigated repeated nightmares and behavioural difficulties among the children. Even in cases where physical force, threats or psychological pressures are not used to persuade children to take part in the production of pornographic images, it should be realized that the status of being a child influences the individual's choice of action. Children are less likely to feel able to say 'no' to an adult, however friendly or trusted that adult may be, than another adult would be in the same position. They are also less able to judge the long- and short-term consequences of their actions.

A further aspect of the production and distribution of child pornography is the effect upon children who are exposed to these products as consumers. Paedophiles frequently use this material to persuade children to perform sexual acts. But children could be exposed to photographic depictions of such acts independently of paedophiles, particularly in countries where pornography is freely available and children's consumption of magazines and videos is unsupervised. There is no adequate research about the effects of pornography on children as consumers. As with the question of child sexual activity, there are those who would argue that because some children experience some material as sexually exciting it is important for child rights that they have access to such material. Thus one psychologist asserts that:

> Were sex sufficiently acceptable so that healthy and affectionate but erotic portrayals of human sexuality became an integral part of children's literature and television, likelihood of interest in, exposure to, or negative effects from poorer pornography would be reduced. Currently the basest and most degrading material is forbidden but available, while affectionate, healthy erotica is censored. (Constantine 1979, p. 506)

The same author suggests that those truly concerned for child welfare would prefer the production of pornography under controlled conditions to the present exploitation of runaways and 'children who are mere chattels of their parents' (p. 507). At the other end of the scale, there are those who would ban even books on sexual education on the grounds not only that they subvert parental control, but also that, because they are illustrated, they 'brutalize sex' for children (*Observer*, London, 20 January 1985).

The fantasy element in child pornography turns upon the concept of childhood. With respect to child pornography, it entails both a symbolic return to the lost childhood of the self (as in paedophilia) and a reprise of the sexual excitement of youth. The desire involved is not an abnormal contradiction of societal norms, as some observers claim (Bat Ada and Densen-Gerber for example) – rather it represents an over-valuation of what Western society values most highly. The preferred sexuality of women in the representations of Western culture is analogous to the helpless sexuality of children: sexuality in need of protection. The attraction appeals to and emphasizes the strength of a protector. It is not difficult to find examples of advertisements which make use of this to sell commodities, whether the model is a child or a woman. There is little doubt that the drawing of a little girl with a ruffled skirt which is used in an OXO advertisement is derived from the same cultural fantasy as the well known image of Marilyn Monroe in the film *Seven Year Itch* (figure 6).

The Western ideal body shape is strikingly reminiscent of adolescence: 'a version of an immature body' (Coward 1984, p. 41). The fact that the body of a child is free from pubic and bodily hair is clearly important for the paedophile market. This factor is stressed continually in advertising copy for the child pornography market. Likewise, in the pages of women's magazines, adult Western women are offered a variety of products for removing body hair in order to achieve a pre-pubescent smoothness. Coward has commented that 'this sexual ideal is an image which connotes power-lessness' (p. 42) and suggests that it means that women have 'a sexuality which pervades their bodies almost as if in spite of themselves' (p. 42). This lack of power as well as the

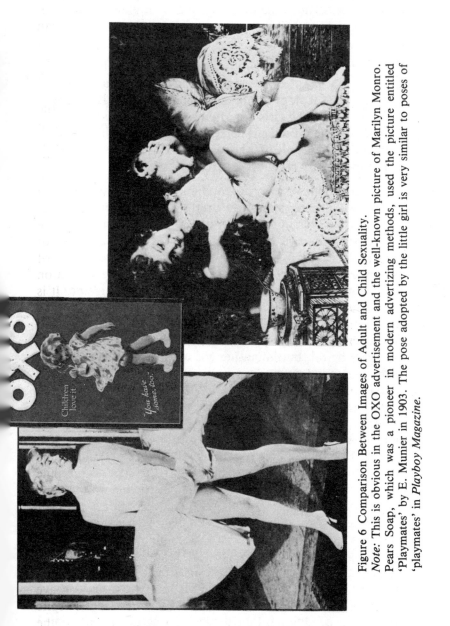

Figure 6 Comparison Between Images of Adult and Child Sexuality.
Note: This is obvious in the OXO advertisement and the well-known picture of Marilyn Monro. Pears Soap, which was a pioneer in modern advertizing methods, used the picture entitled 'Playmates' by E. Munier in 1903. The pose adopted by the little girl is very similar to poses of 'playmates' in *Playboy Magazine*.

attribution of an unconscious sexuality applies to an even greater extent to children, who thus become more attractive to male sexual desire.

> The image is of a highly sexualized female whose sexuality is still one of response *to* the active sexuality of a man. The ideology about adolescent sexuality is exactly the same; young girls are often seen as expressing a sexual need even if the girl herself does not know it. It is an image which feeds off the idea of a fresh, spontaneous, but essentially *responsive* sexuality. (p. 43)

Translated into the pornographic mode, this may appear as a series of photographs of a pretty blonde taken in mock-stately-home surroundings, with a text which reads: 'I remember Krissie, a Nordic beauty in the last fading instant of her innocence. Just 16, she was eternal . . . She was an au pair working for my father Lord Ingleby . . . looking after him, comforting him, fulfilling his every need' (*Penthouse Collection, Special Wedding Edition for Madonna*, vol. 1 no. 3, p. 19). Or, more explicitly, as an advertisement for a film called *Little Nymph* – accompanying a picture showing a post-pubertal, but immature girl astride a young man on a bed: 'A young nympho schoolgirl gives her boyfriend a wonderful orgy . . .'.

A further aspect of the pornographic representation of children is its relationship to the routine use of childish nakedness to advertise consumer products, often as gratuitously as sexual images of women are used to sell unrelated objects like cars or scenery. In view of the type of material described above, one wonders what a paedophile would make of the 'blonde and beefy' child in the advertisement in figure 7. Certainly sex offenders in English prisons have been known to send for *Mothercare* catalogues as stimulants to their obsessive fantasies (Wyre 1985). Childish nakedness is not always innocent in the eye of a beholder. In an ideal world, advertising practice would reconsider the necessity of using naked children to sell commodities; it is part of the oppression of children that they are so used, just as women are oppressed by the same type of mechanism. Nevertheless it is incorrect to consider this as part of a male conspiracy or to conclude that the two oppressions are the same, as Florence Rush does in her condemnation of the 1970 United States Commission on Obscenity and Pornography: '[The Commission's] ability to ignore child pornography could only stem from a conscious or unconscious determination to tolerate male sexual interest in children and not to interfere in the lucrative child pornography industry' (Rush 1980, p. 80). I would argue that the fault is more likely to lie in social misunderstanding of sexuality, combined with an inability to recognize children's rights and the overall ideology of the free market system.

Figure 7 Big, Blonde and Beefy.
Note: What does a paedophile make of the baby in this advertisement?

7

One Child at a Time

I wish either my father or my mother, or indeed both of
them, as they were both equally bound to it, had minded
what they were about when they begot me; had they
then duly considered how much depended upon what
they were then doing.

Laurence Sterne *The Life and Opinions*
of Tristram Shandy

Clinical practitioners in the Western world are gradually
developing an expertise with sexually abused children. The
children seen by paediatricians, psychologists and psy-
chiatrists may be any age from infancy to late adolescence;
the abuse to which they have been subjected can cover a wide
range. It may mean that a baby has been forced to commit
fellatio on its father, or been genitally overstimulated by its
mother. It may be that a boy has been selling sexual services
occasionally in order to buy cocaine; or it may be a girl has
become pregnant by an adult friend of her family. They may
have experienced physical damage or have acquired other
health problems, such as drug abuse, or they may simply be
frightened and confused. Although it may seem that there is
an epidemic in child sexual abuse over the past decade, what
most clinical practitioners seem to be agreed on is that this is
likely to be an effect of an increase in reporting, as was the
case with the 'battered child syndrome', first described by
Henry Kempe just over two decades ago (Kempe et al. 1962;
Krugman 1985). As medical practitioners begin to recognize
the symptoms of child sexual abuse in the child's health and
behaviour, they are developing new methods of treatment
and also passing on their expertise to teachers, parents and
social workers so that they too can be alert to recognizing the
symptoms. Children are also being taught how to recognize,

avoid or reject sexual abuse. This can be done sensitively without producing fear or disgust in the child. Some experiments have already been made with the use of dolls with sexual organs to help children with a limited vocabulary or knowledge to describe what has happened to them. Children are also being taught how to say 'no' to adults. They are being encouraged to discuss their right to express dislike of particular kinds of touching and to recognize which adults to tell about sexual abuse. School programmes have been developed to encourage children to explore ways of avoiding abuse using methods such as role play, and several videos have been produced for sale to parents and schools (Kaplan 1984).

Most cases seen by clinicians involve sexual abuse rather than exploitation for profit. However, popular published accounts tend to stress this less common aspect of exploitation for profit. Some responsible research has helped to counter newspaper scandals. The government of Canada's report on sexual exploitation makes it clear that one of the priorities for prevention is the education of both adults and children about the dangers of child sexual abuse and of prostitution and pornography. The report suggests that Provincial Child Protection Services should be established to meet the needs of young prostitutes and to 'identify the early warning signs of troubled home conditions warranting the provision of special services' (Government of Canada 1984, pp. 50–1). This is sound policy in theory but, as the report itself demonstrates, only about half of all child prostitutes come from recognizably unsuccessful homes. Other suggestions include establishing agencies to provide job training and counselling for young prostitutes, as well as attempts to educate them in life skills, which would help their reintroduction into both the formal labour market and society.

So much depends on the resources and policies of the country involved. Treatment of sexually exploited children varies according to social work principles, attitudes to children and available welfare provision. Most discussion about the treatment of child victims of sexual abuse has taken place in the West, where it is possible to implement decisions to provide more clinical psychologists, special prevention programmes, new clinics and therapy centres. But, in a nation which lacks all but the most basic social welfare provision, social work practices may of necessity be oriented towards control and punishment rather than prevention, rehabilitation and counselling. This is what happened in a Peruvian case of double incest, in which a girl on the threshold of puberty had been having intercourse with her father and her brother over a period of more than a year. This was discovered when she became pregnant and gave birth to a child, without having experienced her first menstrual period. The father was imprisoned and her brother put on probation. The only treatment received by any family member was weekly meetings between the boy and his probation officer, who gave him some talks on the physiology of sex and birth control. The girl continued to live with her mother, her brother and other siblings and her own child. The father's imprisonment was, in fact, a punishment for the whole family. Not only was the household deprived of his potential earnings but they were also expected to provide for his material support while he was in jail (Ennew 1982).

Many experienced practitioners see child sexual abuse as a family problem. There are clear indications that abusers have themselves been abused as children and that what society sees as their offences are the result of this, either within their own family group or, in the case of those who cannot form family relationships, with unrelated children. Incest is seen not only as an offence by an individual, but as part of the web of family relationships, and is treated accordingly (Bentovim 1985). In the intensive social work practices of countries with a developed welfare system, like the United Kingdom, the emphasis in nearly all family problems is on the reconstruction, support or maintenance of the family group. Thus current practice with incest, as with problems like juvenile crime and parental alcohol abuse, is to counsel the family group (Jordan 1972).

Family oriented social work may be aimed at prevention,

by targetting groups felt to be 'at risk', or it may concentrate on families known to have problems, and be rehabilitative. In both cases it is open to criticism because of interference in family privacy and the implications of control by state agencies (Donzelot 1980; Meyer 1977). An alternative is self-help group work, which concentrates on victims. Such approaches are non-statutory, although they may be supported by state funds. In the case of child sexual abuse the work consists of counselling, which aims to deal with long-term effects on adults who were sexually abused as children. The counsellors are all victims themselves and their work as therapists is, to a large extent, part of their own rehabilitation. Groups like the British Incest Survivors Group have been important in breaking the silence about the sexual abuse of children. The evidence of today's adults about their childhood experiences has led to the recognition that child sexual abuse is far more widespread than had previously been admitted. Moreover it has helped today's children by making their complaints credible.

Sereny describes one alternative to family-oriented therapy. At the time when she was researching, the West Berlin authorities encouraged young prostitutes to remain outside their family of origin, if this had proved too difficult an environment for them to cope with. But, unlike United Kingdom social workers, they did not remove the child into state care in an institution or recognized foster home. The young person was given a state income with which to maintain a home, in which he or she was allowed to live with a sexual partner if they wished, provided that they returned to school and continued to attend until they had reached school leaving age (Sereny 1984).

One of the problems with the rehabilitation of young prostitutes is that they have already been socialized into street life and are familiar with criminal pursuits. Some are involved in drug consumption or dealing, others with petty theft, which is often associated with sexual trading. Street life, theft and prostitution all involve a life-style based on short-term gains: rapid cash return for little effort combined with speedy spending on non-durable consumer goods. Rehabilitation schemes have to aim to lead minors to accept the delayed gratification which schooling, training, legitimate employ-ment and mature relationships demand (Braun 1982).

In the developing world, rehabilitation may be almost entirely in the hands of voluntary agencies and this has led to some innovative approaches. The Udada Club in Nairobi was founded by accident, when a Catholic missionary offered a meal to a girl prostitute he had encountered in the street. When she returned in the company of 23 colleagues, the Father decided to found a community to help them. By 1981 the Club had grown to a membership of 60 girls, aged between 13 and 16. A three-year training programme had been devised in which they were taught to read in Swahili and English, and trained in basic domestic tasks. The aim of the project is to give the girls a chance to return to 'normal life. They are not given sermons about the sins of prostitution and are under no obligation to complete the programme. Some do return to the streets, but they are not necessarily regarded as failures (Kabeba 1981).

As yet there are no experts in the cross-cultural dimen-sions of child sexual exploitation and abuse, and this sort of perspective is vital since so many who write about this theme discuss it in terms of human universals. Wherever work has been done it tends to be patchy, anecdotal and journalistic. Sometimes work on prostitutes only incidentally touches on children, often it only deals with one aspect of the problem and only very seldom does it try to place that aspect within the context of the social and sexual relations of which it is a part. One of my strongest impressions after researching and writing this book is that the sexual exploitation of children is less a set of abnormal practices than an extreme manifesta-tion of prevailing social and sexual values.

Although I have said that the evidence is patchy, this should not be taken to mean that there is no literature on the subject. As Bo Carlsson found when he researched the sub-ject, the literature is enormous. He produced a 60-page bibliography which my research assistant and I increased by two-thirds after only a few weeks' work. But the problems in making sense of all this published and unpublished material are that none of it is comparative, the methodology is often defective, and it still leaves huge gaps in our knowledge. Nevertheless it is still possible to make some general, if tentative, conclusions.

First I would draw attention to the proposition that child sexual exploitation and abuse can only be understood in the context of two sets of power relations: those between men and women, and between adults and children, complicated by race and class. This is most clearly seen in the case of sex tourism where youth submits to age and female to male, while the inequality between inhabitants of rich and poor nations is combined with racial and ethnic discrimination. The two poles of the nexus are represented by rich, white, adult Western males and poor, non-white, young, non-Western females. But the most important fact for child sexual exploitation is that the concept of child rights is so little discussed. In many societies, including our own, adult power over children is so absolute that in a sense all children are abused and all adults are abusers.

The second point is what I think of as the 'white slavery' effect. A great deal of literature about child sexual exploitation ignores the importance of placing the data in context or even of working through the difficult process of data collection, verification and analysis. It starts from the proposition that we know what child sexual exploitation is, asserts that it is increasing rapidly, then gives a single reason for both occurrence and increase. The reasons offered fall into two main categories. Put bluntly, these are: (1) the family is breaking down due to permissiveness and enormous vice rings which threaten to corrupt all young people; (2) child sexual exploitation is part of the oppression of women by men and includes a vast traffic in women and children, which is operated by vice rings.

These two points of view are relatively antagonistic in their political outcomes, but similar in their approach to evidence and modes of argument. I would contend that they exploit the data for political ends and thus exploit the children whose stories are caught up in it. Both lines of argument, together with many researchers, use terms like 'Baby Pros', 'Kiddie Porn' and 'the Meat Rack' when they refer to these children, with intent to shock and draw attention to their cause. They also tend to exaggerate figures or use them in ways which are statistically unviable, ignoring for instance the fact that the apparent increase in sexual abuse in North America and Europe is due to an increase in reporting and not, necessarily, of incidence.

Against arguments about increased permissiveness it must be stated that the 'family' is not breaking down. It is changing, but family form has always changed to fit different circumstances. The work of the Cambridge Group for the History of Population has shown that there never has been a 'golden age' of the Family to provide a traditional ideal (e.g. Laslett et al. 1980). In addition, a great deal of anthropological literature indicates that different forms of family life are successful in nurturing and socializing children. When the idea of vice rings and stranger abuse is publicized in this way it obscures one vitally important fact – the vast amount of child sexual abuse that we know of happens in the family context, either with members of the child's own family, or with people known to the family. This is true for the United States and European countries, and my research in Peru indicates that the same is probably true of less industrialized countries also. Exaggeration of stranger abuse and vice rings obscures the problems within family life and thus leaves many children more at risk of abuse.

Feminist argument may be marred by some of the same errors and, in addition, make the incorrect assumption that children's rights can be secured through the medium of women's rights. This refusal to disaggregate the two groups has two effects. It continues the association between women and children, which is one of the buttresses of male power, and it fails to recognize the importance of sexual exploitation of power relations based on age – the difficulty which a child experiences in saying 'no' to an adult. It also leaves the sexual problems of masculinity untouched. We know that most, but not all, sexual abuse of children is done by men, but this does not mean that all men are child molesters. It simply tells us that a certain number of men are unable to find gratification in mature sexual relationships with a peer. It may indicate that socialization into masculinity is fraught with difficulties, just as feminist theory and practice has demonstrated to be the case with socially acceptable femininity. Many feminist groups campaigning against the sexual exploitation of children ignore the fact that many child prostitutes are male and that little boys are often subjected to sexual abuse. In Cambridge, as I write, there are a number of posters advertising an Incest Survivors Help Group. They say 'All women welcome'. Where do men who were abused as boys turn for help? Research shows that abusers have more often than not been abused themselves as children. Without facing up to their problems, how can we stop the abuse continuing into further generations?

Many publicists of child sexual exploitation, whether taking the perspective of family morality or feminism, assert the existence of profitable vice rings and an international traffic in children, often using unsubstantiated accounts and anecdotes to build their powerful mythologies. Over the past year I have had the unpleasant task of sifting through many reports of vice rings and traffic. I have no doubt that some cases exist, although I have seen none which are conclusively proven. But I have no doubt also that they are not vast, they are not hugely profitable and that exaggeration about them does a disservice to the children in petty, sordid relationships which are the day-to-day reality of the majority of cases of child sexual abuse and exploitation. It seems to me that there is little, or nothing, to be gained from publicizing child abuse by reports of gross numbers. Surely it is sorrow enough to know that one child is being sexually abused, or that one child is living on the streets and selling its sexuality. If there are two, or three, or three thousand it is unbearable knowledge. We should not need figures of hundreds of thousands to act, or to call upon authority to remove the burden of guilt. The child we see, or know to be in danger is our real responsibility, a fact which media campaigns and prurient articles obscure from us.

Despite the arguments against so much publicity, there is no reason to suggest that child sexual abuse and exploitation should be relegated to silence. On the contrary, it is the sort of topic which must be brought to public awareness and form the subject for moral debate. The argument I have used throughout this book has been based on an attempt to examine the evidence about child sexual exploitation. But moral debate cannot be based on mere empirical data, however incontrovertible that data might be. In the process of moral decision making most people probably implicitly or explicitly derive their principles from a relatively coherent framework, like religion, or a political creed, which makes sense to them and to their social group. Although it is often claimed that coherent systems may be repressive, or are more likely to be right-wing, there is more reason for those who are trying to establish egalitarian social rules to establish at the same time a moral rationality (see for example Shapiro 1985).

At the moment it is difficult to take a moral stance on child sexual exploitation, or sexual issues in general, without being forced to choose between one of three philosophies. In one of these, moral absolutism asserts that morals are based on the natural existence of the patriarchal family, and morality in general is reduced to sexual morality in particular. This shrinks the moral sphere to the household level, removing such questions as relationship between nations, treatment of offenders, and the actions of leaders to a higher order political sphere, in which compromise is not only allowed but expected, and from which ordinary people are excluded. Moral decisions become small-scale and personal. Opposed to this are liberationist philosophies, which accord moral priority to individual desires and freedoms, or a philosophy which asserts the essential moral superiority of women.

In this maelstrom of debate between those who favour the patriarchal family and feminists, or between family moralists and the sexual counter-culture, children seem to have little space accorded to them, even though they are the subject of the arguments. There also seems to be limited space for those who are not moral absolutists of one kind or another. If one is not tied to these simplistic, single-cause theories it is easy to see that repression is very different from discipline or that liberation is not the same as permissiveness.

One of the major stumbling-blocks in modern debates about sexual morality is the clash between the importance accorded to individual freedoms and the needs of certain classes of person to be protected. Thus censorship of pornography, even child pornography, is seen as a violation of the rights of the purchaser of pornographic goods. But the rights being asserted here are citizen's rights against the state, rather than the human rights supposedly conferred by nature, and there is no logical reason why citizen's rights cannot be given a priority ranking. Thus the right to protection from damage by exploitation might be agreed to have priority over the right not to have one's sexual enjoyment limited.

If generalized exploitation, rather even than sexual exploitation, were to become the accepted criterion for legislation, then it might be possible to argue for at least two measures to be taken which could limit child sexual exploitation. The first would be a prohibition on the gratuitous use of sexual images for selling any kind of commodity. The second would be a prohibition on the use of real people (adults or children of any sex) in sexual images, but this would only deal with part of the problem. There can be no censorship of fantasy. Thus so long as there are psychologically damaged adult human beings, and children and photographs of children, societies will have to face up to the problem of how to deal with adult–child sexual activities.

One factor which all absolutists have in common is the proposition that sexual instincts are overpowering. According to moral campaigners they must be controlled externally, because they are so overwhelming. Men are unable to control them, according to feminists, and, from the point of view of the sexual counter-culture, the individual's physical and moral health is endangered if they are not indulged. Perhaps all points of view would be better advised to admit that, while sexuality is powerful, it is neither paramount nor uncontrollable. Perhaps they would also be more socially appropriate if they paid attention to the rights of children who are, in the last analysis, the reason for sexual instincts, even if they are not or should not always be the result of sexual activity. What is needed is careful, considered and professional work, like that of David Finkelhor (1979; 1984; 1985) which looks at the problem in the context of children's rights, and of actual clinical experience and sociological data, and considers the abuser not as a monster but as a person – a damaged person. This should be combined with work with an anthropological perspective, like the collection recently edited by Jill E. Korbin, which looks at child abuse in a cross-cultural perspective (Korbin 1981).

We need to make careful distinctions between pre- and post-pubertal abuse and exploitation. We also need to examine sexual values and customs (including our own) before we start research. We have to stop looking only at pathological cases and problem families and use proper methodologies to compare clinical cases with children who have not been abused. We must move away from publicizing the problem either through anecdote or through numbers. It is not helpful to children to use a single case to shock, without examining that example in context. It is not helpful either to talk of thousands or millions of cases, using guestimates rather than statistics. There is a very important sense in which we must examine this problem one child at a time, always remembering that no child exists separately from society, which defines what childhood is and determines how it is experienced.

The basis of infancy and childhood lies in believing what one is told and doing what one is told, while gradually building up a personal picture of social life and social rules. What one believes, receives or conceptualizes is always partial and dependent on context. The environment in which childhood is experienced depends on a combination of generalized cultural factors, and the particular rules and habits of the family or other socialization agencies.

The gradually constructed world view of a child is partial because adults, who transmit it, only have partial knowledge themselves, and because they only impart certain aspects, and do this unsystematically. Many adults are poor communicators and children frequently lack contextualization for information they receive. They also do not have the tools with which to judge the relative weight of contradictory or apparently contradictory messages.

Childhood is a time for forming hypotheses with this variety of informations and putting up barriers against impossible or painful contradictions. In adolescence, hypotheses are tested and further barriers erected when failure results. Early adulthood – often the whole of adult life – is often a fight to maintain both hypotheses and barriers in the face of overwhelming and contradictory evidence. This is what makes the Mexican poet and diplomat, Octavio Paz (1979, p. 43), write 'I have spent the second part of my life breaking the stones, drilling the walls, smashing the doors and removing the obstacles I placed between the light and myself in the first part of my life'. It is not very surprising that moral decisions are difficult to take and that moral debates are frequently conducted through the media of stereotype and heated assertion.

Surely we need to return to, and re-evaluate, moral considerations of all kinds. We need to broaden the sphere of morality to take into consideration all practices which involve a lack of respect for persons: systems of race, class, age and gender – in short, all inequalities and aggressions. A moral society would be a just system which eliminated inequality while acknowledging and catering for difference and variety. If moral debate is reduced to sexual matters, then all other inequalities are bound to be obscured by insistent screams of shock and horror – by exaggeration and distortion. As long as that process continues, children will be exploited sexually, racially, through their poverty, or simply because they are children.

Bibliography

Ageton S. S. 1983. *Sexual Assault Among Adolescents*, Gower Publishing Co. Ltd, Lexington, Mass.

Allen E. E. 1981. 'Testimony before the Committee on the Judiciary United States Senate 1981', by Ernest E. Allen, Chairman of Jefferson County Task Force on Child Prostitution and Pornography.

Alvés-Milho E. 1977. 'El problema de la Prostitución en Iquitos', BA Thesis in Social Work, Catholic University of Lima.

Amnesty International 1985. *Peru Report*, London.

Ansell J. 1984. 'Problems of Prostitution', paper presented to the 28th Congress of the International Abolitionist Federation, Vienna.

Anti-Slavery Society 1984. 'Children in Especially Difficult Circumstances: Child Labour', Report for UNICEF; unpublished manuscript.

Anti-Slavery Society 1985. 'Children in Especially Difficult Circumstances: Street Children', Report for UNICEF, unpublished manuscript.

Aries P. 1973. *Centuries of Childhood: a Social History of Family Life*, Alfred Knopf, New York.

Arnold K. 1978. 'The Whore in Peru', in Lipshitz S (ed.), *Tearing the Veil: Essays in Femininity*, Routledge and Kegan Paul, London.

Asian Women's Liberation 1980. no. 3, *Prostitution Tourism*, Japan.

Asian Women's Liberation 1984. no. 6, *Sex Tourism and Military Occupation,* Japan.

Baker C. D. 1980. 'Preying on Playgrounds', in Schultz L. G. (ed.), 1980.

Banerjee S. 1980. *Child Labour in Thailand*, The Anti-Slavery Society, London.

Barry K. 1979. *Female Sexual Slavery*, Prentice-Hall, New York.

Barry K. 1984. Opening paper: International Politics of Female Slavery', in Barry et al. (eds) 1984.

Barry K., Bunch C. and Castley S. (eds) 1984. *International Feminism: Networking against Female Slavery: Report of the Global Feminist Workshop to Organise against Traffic in Women*, Rotterdam, The Netherlands 6–15 April 1983, published in the USA.

Becerra G. 1985. 'Menores Abandonados en la Calle, Ministry of Justice, Peru.

Bentovim A. 1985. Verbal evidence in interview with child and family psychiatrist at Great Ormond Street Children's Hospital, for TV EYE documentary film *Men Who Molest Children*.

Bhalerao V. R. 1984. 'STD in Child Prostitutes in Bombay', in Naidu U. et al. (eds) 1984. *Child Labour and Health,* Tata Institute of Social Sciences, Bombay, India.

Bond T. 1981. Press Conference of 16 June 1981, Geneva (reproduced by Terre des Hommes, Lausanne Switzerland, mimeo).

Boudhiba A. 1982. *Exploitation of Child Labour; Final Report of the Special Rapporteur of the UN Sub-Commission on Prevention of Discrimination and Protection of Minorities* UN, Geneva.

Bowlby J. 1965. *Child Care and the Growth of Love,* second edition, Penguin, Harmondsworth.

Braun P. 1982. 'Dès moins de 15 ans se prostituent en France', in *Femme et Monde* no. 57.

Bridel R. 1982. 'Traffic of Children', MSS in files of Defence for Children International, Switzerland.

Bridge P. 1978. 'What parents should know and do about "Kiddie Porn"', *Parents Magazine* (USA), January.

Brown B. 1981. 'A Feminist Interest in Pornography – Some Modest Proposals', in *M/F* nos 5 and 6.

Campagna D. 1985. 'The Economics of Juvenile Prostitution in the USA', in *International Children's Rights Monitor* vol. 2 no. 1.

Carlsson B. 1984. 'The Sexual Exploitation of Children', unpublished draft manuscript for the Anti-Slavery Society, London.

Catholic Social Welfare Commission 1977. Evidence Submitted to the Home Office Committee appointed in September 1977.

Children's Legal Centre 1985. *Briefing: Young People's Rights and the Gillick Case*, London.

'Christiane F.' 1980. *'H': Autobiography of a Child Prostitute and Heroin Addict*, Corgi Books, UK.

Claire R. and Cottingham J. 1984. 'Migration and Tourism: an overview', in *Women and Development*, ISIS, Switzerland.

Comer L. 1979. 'Ideology of Child Care', in Hoyles M. (ed.) 1977.

Constantine L. L. 1979. 'The Sexual Rights of Children: Implications of a Radical Perspective', in Cook and Wilson (eds) 1979.

Cook M. and Wilson G. (eds) 1979. *Love and Attraction: An International Conference*, Pergamon Press, Oxford.

Coward R. 1978. 'The Making of the Feminine', *Spare Rib* no. 70, May.

Coward R. 1984. *Female Desire*, Paladin, London.

Creatividad y Cambio 1981. 'La Prostitución: Símbolo de la Condición Femenina', *Creatividad y Cambio*, Lima, Peru.

Davidson H. A. 1982. 'Sexual Exploitation of Children in the United States': paper presented to the 4th International Congress on Child Abuse and Neglect, Paris, 1982.

Davidson M. 1962. *The World, the Flesh and Myself*, Arthur Barker Ltd., London.

Davidson S. 1982. 'Lust City in the Far East', in *Time*, 10 May.

Degérando, Baron J–M 1824. *Considerations sur les Methodes a suivre dans l'Observation des Peuples Sauvages,* Société de l'observateurs de l'Homme, Paris.

Donzelot J. 1980. *The Policing of Families,* Hutchinson, UK.

Driver E. 1985. 'Child Abuse: Breaking the Silence', *New Statesman*, 11 January.

Dudar H. 1977. 'America Discovers Child Pornography', in *MS*, August.

Dworkin A. 1981. *Pornography*, Women's Press, London.

ECOSOC 1984. Review of Developments in the field of Slavery and the Slave Trade in all their Practices and Manifestations. Reports by States concerning the Convention for the Suppression of the Traffic in Persons and the Exploitation of the Prostitution of Others. Note by the Secretary General E/CN.4/Sub.2/AC.2/1984/5, 17 May, Geneva.

Eiduson B. T. and Alexander J. W. 1978. 'The Role of Children in Alternative Family Styles', in *Journal of Social Issues* vol. 34 no. 2.

'Elisabeth and Ruth' 1977. 'Changing with my Daughter', in *Spare Rib* no. 60, July.

English Collective of Prostitutes, New York Prostitutes Collective, US Prostitutes Collective 1981. 'Nos besoins, nos desirs, nos revindications . . .'; document submitted in French to the 27th Congress of the International Abolitionist Federation, 8 September.

Ennew J. 1982. 'International Adoption: a Case Study of Peru', report for the Anti-Slavery Society.

Ennew J. 1985a. 'Juvenile Street Workers in Lima, Peru', unpublished report for the Overseas Development Administration and the Anti-Slavery Society.

Ennew J. 1985b. 'Child Workers: Serving or Working?', *International Children's Rights Monitor* vol. 2 no. 2.

Ennew J. 1986. 'Libertad Vigilada', unpublished report for the Peruvian Juvenile Probation Service.

Fernand-Laurent J. 1983. 'Report of the Special Rapporteur on the Suppression of the Traffic in Persons and the Exploitation of the Prostitution of Others', ECOSOC E/1983/7 17 March, United Nations, Geneva.

Finkelhor D. 1979. 'What's wrong with sex between adults and children? Ethics and the problem of sexual abuse', in *American Journal of Orthopsychiatry* vol. 49 no. 4.

Finkelhor D., Gelles R. J., Hotlaing G. T. & Strauss M. A.

1983. *The Dark Side of the Family*, Sage Publications, Beverly Hills.

Firestone S. 1971. *The Dialectic of Sex*, Jonathan Cape, USA.

Foucault M. 1979. *The History of Sexuality*, Allen Lane, London.

Frank E. P. 1977. 'What are they doing to our children?', in *Good Housekeeping*, August, p. 99.

Fuller P. 1979. 'Uncovering Childhood', in Hoyles M. (ed.) 1979.

Gersen R. L. 1979. *The Hidden Victims: the Sexual Abuse of Children*, Beacon Press, Boston, USA.

Giovannoni J. M. and Becerra R. M. 1979. *Defining Child Abuse*, The Free Press, New York, USA.

Goethe J. W. 1970. *Italian Journey*, Penguin, Harmondsworth.

Goodman J. 1985. 'The Flowering of Brooke Shields', in *Company*, September.

Goodwin J. 1982. *Sexual Abuse: Incest Victims and Their Families*, John Wright PSG Inc, USA.

Gordon R. 1976. 'Paedophilia: Normal and Abnormal', in Kraemer W. (ed.) 1976.

Gorky M. 1966. *My Childhood*, Penguin, Harmondsworth.

Government of Canada 1984. 'Summary of Sexual Offences against Children in Canada'; report of the Committee on Sexual Offences Against Children and Youths: appointed by the Minister of Justice and Attorney General of Canada, the Minister of National Health and Welfare.

Government of Jamaica 1978. National Planning Agency: Five Year Development Plan 1978–82, Main Document.

Gray G. Z. 1871. *The Children's Crusade*, London, referred to in Hoyles 1979.

Gray P. 1973. 'Turning Out: a Study of Teenage Prostitution', in *Urban Life and Culture*, January pp. 401–42.

Hastrup K. 1978. in Ardener S. (ed.) *Defining Females*, Croom Helm, London.

Heid Bracey D. 1979. *Baby-Pros, preliminary profiles of juvenile prostitutes*, John Jay Press, New York.

Hernandez Aguilar Z. and del Pozo T. 1967. 'Rasgos Psicológicos Predominantes en las Madres Prostitutas'; paper presented to UNICEF seminar in Lima, 'La Familia, Infancia y Juventud en el Desarollo Nacional'.

Hoelgaard S. 1984. 'The Foster Care Triad: Structure and Process', Ph.D Thesis in Social Anthropology, University of Cambridge.

Honoré R. 1978. *Sex Law*, Duckworth, UK.

Hoyles M. (ed.) 1979. *Changing Childhood*, Writers and Readers Publishing Cooperative, London.

Hunt D. 1970. *Parents and Children in History*, Basic Books, New York.

Huxley A. 1971. *The Devils of Loudun*, Penguin, Harmondsworth.

Illinois Legislature Investigation Commission 1980. *Sexual Exploitation of Children*; a report of the Illinois General Assembly, State of Illinois, USA.

Irigary L. 1977. Ce sexe qui n'en es pas un, Éditions de Minuit, Paris, France.

Ismodes A. 1967. 'Prostitución en Lima', paper presented to UNICEF Seminar, La 'Familia, Infancia y Juventud en el Desarollo Nacional'.

Jamaica Tourist Board 1978. *Travel Statistics Jamaica*, mimeo.

Janus S. S. and Heid Bracey D. H. 1980. *Runaways – Pornography and prostitution*, mimeo, New York, USA.

Johnson S. 1775. *A Journey to the Western Isles of Scotland*, 2 vols, A. Leatherley and J. Exshaw, Dublin.

Jordan W. 1972. *The Social Worker in the Family*, Routledge and Kegan Paul, London.

Kabeba I. 1981. 'Offering Alternatives', in *Ideas Forum* no. 16, UNICEF.

Kaiser E. 1981. 'La Prostitution Enfantine Exportée d'Europe au "Tiers Monde"', mimeo, Terre des Hommes, Lausanne.

Kaplan D. 1984. 'Facing up to Sex Abuse', in *Time*, 12 December, USA.

Kapur P. 1978. *The Life and World of Call-Girls in India:*

a sociopsychological study of the artistocratic prostitute, Vikas Publishing House PVT Ltd, New Delhi.

Karunatilleke K. 1981. 'Recent trends in the fight against the traffic in human beings and the exploitation of prostitution, paper submitted on behalf of INTERPOL to the 27th Congress of the International Abolitionist Federation, Nice, France.

Kempe C. H. and R. E. Helfer (eds) 1980. *The Battered Child*, 3rd edition. University of Chicago Press.

Kinsey A. C., Pomeroy W. B. and Martin C. E. 1948. *Sexual behaviour in the human male*, W. B. Saunders, Philadelphia.

Korbin J. E. 1981. *Child Abuse and Neglect: Cross-Cultural Perspectives*, University of California Press.

Kraemer W. 1976. 'A Paradise Lost', in Kraemer W. (ed.) *The Forbidden Love: The Normal and Abnormal Love of Children*, Sheldon Press, London.

Krugman R. 1985. 'Child Abuse in Industrial Societies', paper presented to the XIXth CIOMS Conference on Battered Children and Child Abuse, Berne, Switzerland 4–6 December.

Langfeldt T. 1979. 'Processes in Sexual development', in Cook and Wilson (eds) 1979.

Laslett P., Ooesterveen K. and Smith R. M. (eds) 1980. *Bastardy and its Comparative History*, Edward Arnold, London.

Lebra J. and Paulson J. 1980. *Chinese Women in South East Asia*, Times Books International, Singapore.

Lederer L. (ed.) 1980. *Take Back the Night*, Morrow & Co., New York.

Lee C. 1985. 'Victory for Mrs Gillick is a Tragedy for Thousands of Young People', in *The Guardian*, 30 January p. 22.

Lee L. 1962. *Cider with Rosie*, Penguin, Harmondsworth.

Levi-Strauss C. 1969. *The Elementary Structures of Kinship*, Eyre and Spottiswode, London.

Lindsey K. 1976. 'Madonna or Whore?', in *Sister Courage*, March.

Lloyd R. 1979. *Playland: a Study of Human Exploitation*, Blond and Briggs, London.

McCall C. n/d. 'An Angry Doctor Battles Against a Gruesome Black Market in Asian Children; xerox of article: in files of Defence for Children International, Switzerland.

McCleod E. 1982. *Women Working: Prostitution Now*, Croom Helm, London.

McIntosh P. 1984. 'Baby of schoolgirl', in *Archives of Disease in Childhood* vol. 59, October pp. 915–17.

Manazan Sr. M. J. 1982. 'Sexual Exploitation in a Third World Setting', MSS in files of Defence for Children International, Switzerland.

Mann T. 1979. *Death in Venice*, Secker & Warbug/Octopus, London.

Martinson F. M. 1979. 'Infant and Child Sexuality: Capacity and Experience', in Cook and Wilson (eds) 1979.

Matsui Y. 1980. 'Economy and Psychology of Prostitution and Tourism', in Asian Women's Liberation, 1980.

Mause L. de (ed.) 1979. *The History of Childhood*, Souvenir Press.

Mead M. 1942. *Growing Up in New Guinea*, Penguin, Harmondsworth.

Mead M. 1955. 'Theoretical Setting 1954', in Mead M. and Wolfstein M. (eds) 1955 *Childhood in Contemporary Culture*, Phoenix Books, University of Chicago Press.

Mead M. 1962. *Male and Female*, Pelican, London.

Meyer P. 1977. *L'Enfant et la Raison d'Etat,* Editions de la Maison des Sciences de l'Homme, Paris.

Millet K. 1971. *Sexual Politics*, Abacus.

Morin S. F. and Schultz S. J. 1978. 'The Gay Movement and the Rights of Children', in *The Journal of Social Issues* vol. 34 no. 2.

Morris M. 1984. 'Jolly hockeysticks at adults village school', in *The Guardian*, 3 April.

Moselina L. 1978. 'Rest and Recreation: the US Naval base at Subic Bay', in *ISIS*, Switzerland 13 pp. 17–20.

O'Carroll T. 1980. *Paedophilia: the Radical Case*, Alyson Publishers, Boston, USA.

O'Grady R. (ed.) 1980. *Third World Tourism: Report of a Workshop on Tourism held in Manila*, September 12–25, Christian Conference of Asia.

Ohse U. 1984. *Forced Prostitution and Traffic in Women in West Germany*, Human Rights Group, Edinburgh.

Paz O. 1979. *Selected Poems*, translated by Charles Tomlinson, Penguin, Harmondsworth.

Péron M. F. 1808. 'Voyages de découvertes aux terres Australies', vol. 1, 2 and Atlas, J. Milbert, Paris.

Perpignan Sr. M–S. 1981. 'Prostitution Tourism', in World Council of Churches, *Women in a Changing World: Prostution and Tourism* no. 11, December.

Perpignan Sr. M–S. 1983. *Philippine Women in the Service and Entertainment Sector*; TWMAEW, Singapore.

Pescatello A. (ed.) 1980. *Female and Male in Latin America*, University of Pittsburgh Press.

Pestalozzi H. 1981. L'enfant et la publicité', in *Pro Juventude Monthly Review* nos 1–3, Zurich, Switzerland.

Pinard-Legry J–L. and Lapouge B. 1980. *L'enfant et le pedéraste*, Editions du Seuil, Paris.

Platt A. 1969. *The Child Savers: The Invention of Delinquency*, University of Chicago Press.

Plumb J. H. 1972. 'Children: the Victims of Time', in Plumb J. H. (ed.) *The Light of History* Allen Lane, London.

Portugal A. M. 1982. 'Déjenos ser bellas!', in *Diario la Marka*, 12 July p. 10.

Pottisham Weiss N. 1978. 'Mother–Child Dyad Revisited', in *The Journal of Social Issues* vol. 34 no. 2.

Redley S. 1984. 'Horror of Sex for Sale Boys', in *Northamptonshire Post*, 25 October p. 5.

Robertson S. I. 1983. 'The Needs of the Sexually Abused Child', in *Australian Paediatric Journal* no. 19.

Roe C. 1911. *The Great War on White Slavery*, reprinted in 1979 by Garland Publishing Inc., New York and London.

Rosen R. 1982. *The Lost Sisterhood: Prostitution in America 1900–1918*, The Johns Hopkins Press, Baltimore and London.

Rossman P. 1979. *Sexual Experience between Men and Boys*, Maurice, Temple Smith Ltd., London.

Rush R. 1980. 'Child Pornography', in Lederer L. (ed.) 1980.

Russianoff P. (ed.) 1981. *Women in Crisis*, Human Science Press, New York.

Schultz L. G. (ed.) 1980. *The Sexual Victimology of Youth*, Charles C. Thomas, Springfield, USA.

Sereny G. 1984. *The Invisible Children: a Study of Child Prostitution*, Andre Deutsch, London.

Shapiro R. 1985. 'Britain's Sexual Counter-Revolutionaries', in *Marxism Today* vol. 29 no. 2, February.

Sieghart P. 1985. *The Lawful Rights of Mankind*, Oxford University Press.

Silbert M. H. n/d. 'Prostitution and Sexual assault: Summary of results', mimeo from Delaney Street Foundation Inc., San Francisco, USA.

Simeral I. 1916. *Reform Movements on Behalf of Children in England in the Early Nineteenth Century, and the Agents of those Reforms*, Clifton, New Jersey.

Skolnik A. and Skolnik J. 1971. *Family and Marriage in Transition: Rethinking Marriage, Sexuality, Child Rearing and Family Organisation*, Little and Brown, Boston, USA.

SOS Enfants 1981. 'Dossier d'information sur la prostitution et la pornographie des énfants mineurs de deux sexes', Mimeo.

Spartacus 1980. *Spartacus Holiday Help Portfolio: Manila*, Spartacus, Amsterdam.

Stern M. and Stern A. 1979. *Sex in the Soviet Union*, W. H. Allen, London.

Stier S. 1978. 'Children's Rights and Society's Duties', in *The Journal of Social Issues* vol. 34 no. 2.

Swift C. 1978. 'Sexual assault of Children and Adolescents', Testimony to the House of Representatives, 11 January.

Taylor D. 1984. 'Kiss daddy goodnight', in *New Internationalist* no. 138 pp. 26–7.

Taylor F. 1975. *Jamaica – the Welcoming Society: Myths and Reality*, Institute of Social and Economic research,

University of the West Indies, Monba, Jamaica Working Paper no. 5.

Thornberry T. P. and Silverman R. A. 1971. 'Exposure to pornography and juvenile delinquency, the relationship indicated by juvenile court records'; Technical Report of the Commission on Obscenity and Pornography, Preliminary Studies vol. 1 pp. 178–9, Washington DC, US Government Printing Office.

Turner L. and Ash J. 1975. *The Golden Hordes: International Tourism and the Pleasure Periphery,* Constable, London.

Tyler T. 1982. 'Child Pornography: the International Exploitation of Children', paper presented to the 4th International Congress on Child Abuse and Neglect.

URSA 1981. 'Adolescent Male Prostitution: a study of sexual exploitation, etiological factors and runaway behaviour'; Draft of Executive Summary, California, October.

Vice Commission of Chicago 1911. 'The Social Evil in Chicago: A study of Existing Conditions with Recommendations', Gunthrop Warren, Chicago, reprinted in Roe C. 1911.

Vizard E. 1984. 'The Sexual Abuse of Children'; parts 1 and 2 in *Health Visitor* no. 157.

Voltaire 1971. *Philosophical Dictionary,* Penguin, Harmondsworth.

Wapshott N. 1984. 'Jodie Foster Grows Up', in *Observer Colour Supplement*, 2 December.

Washburn C. K. 1983. 'A Feminist Analysis of Child Abuse and Neglect', in Finkelhor et al. (eds) 1983.

Weeks J. 1985. 'Putting the Sex into Socialism', *New Statesman*, 8 February.

Wharton W. J. L. (ed.) 1893. *Captain Cook's Journal during his First Voyage around the World made in HM Bark Endeavour 1768–71, a literal transcription of the original manuscript,* Elliot Stock, London.

Wihtol R. 1982. 'Hospitality Girls in the Manila Tourist Belt', in *Philippine Journal of Industrial Relations* vol. vi nos 1–2.

Williams M. 1976. 'A Struggle for Normality', in Kraemer W. (ed.) 1976.

Williams Report 1979. Report of the Committee on Obscenity and Film Censorship, HMSO, November 1979 and *Cmnd* 7772.

Wollen P. 1979. 'Do children really need toys?' in Hoyles (ed.) 1979.

Wyden P. and Wyden B. 1968. *Growing up Straight*, Stein and Day, New York.

Wyre R. 1985. Verbal evidence given in interview by Probation Officer for Albany Prison for TV EYE documentary film *Men Who Molest Children*.

Index